SOCIAL MEDIA AND SOCIAL WORK

Implications and Opportunities for Practice

Edited by
Claudia Megele and Peter Buzzi

First published in Great Britain in 2020 by

Policy Press
University of Bristol
1-9 Old Park Hill
Bristol
BS2 8BB
UK
t: +44 (0)117 954 5940
pp-info@bristol.ac.uk
www.policypress.co.uk

British Library Cataloguing in Publication Data
A catalogue record for this book is available from the British Library.

ISBN 978-1-4473-2739-4 paperback
ISBN 978-1-4473-2741-7 ePub
ISBN 978-1-4473-2740-0 ePdf

Policy Press works to counter discrimination on grounds of gender, race, disability, age and sexuality.

Cover design by Clifford Hayes
Cover image credit: melpomen (image from 123rf)
Printed and bound in Great Britain by CMP, Poole
Policy Press uses environmentally responsible print partners

Contents

List of figures and tables iv
A note from the editors to the reader v
Notes on contributors vi

1 Introduction 1
Claudia Megele and Peter Buzzi
2 Digital professionalism and social media ethics 19
Claudia Megele and Peter Buzzi
3 Social media and social work with children and young people and looked after children 61
Claudia Megele and Sherry Malik
4 Social media and adult social work 93
Peter Buzzi and Sharon Allen
5 Social media and mental health social work 113
Ruth Allen and Peter Buzzi
6 Social media and youth justice: challenges and possibilities for practice 133
Naomi Thompson and Ian Joseph
7 Social media and 'communities of practice' and 'communities of interest' 155
Claudia Megele and Peter Buzzi
8 Social media and social work regulation 177
Claudia Megele, Lyn Romeo and Peter Buzzi
9 Future technology and social work and social care practice and education 207
Claudia Megele and Peter Buzzi

Index 221

List of figures and tables

Figures

2.1 Components of digital professionalism 24
2.2 Domains of information sharing 31
2.3 Social Media and Activity Reflection Tool (SMART) 35
2.4 Social Media Activity and Reflection Tool (SMART) mapping example 40
2.5 Knowledge and skills for digital citizenship and digital professionalism 48
2.6 Digital capabilities for digital professionalism 50
3.1 Assessment diamond or assessment square for holistic safeguarding of children and young people 63
4.1 UK adults' use of internet 95
7.1 The @SWSCmedia's reflective cycle of knowledge generation 161

Tables

4.1 Use of social media platforms by practitioners to contact or communicate with service users 98
6.1 Results of the One Big Debate Survey 145
9.1 The impact of the web and digital and social media technologies 210

A note from the editors to the reader

From everyday communication to online shopping and from online games and entertainment to finding employment or remote working, people use digital technologies for everyday purposes and to meet their needs. In this sense, digital technologies have transformed and reshaped the way we work, communicate, connect and relate to each other and this has direct implications for social work and social care practice. In spite of this, findings from the national research on digital professionalism and online safeguarding by the Principal Children and Families Social Worker (PCFSW) network highlight significant inequalities and the need for evidence-based training and development in digital practice skills and online safeguarding across the country.

As always, practitioners are the unsung heroes of social work and social care who during COVID-19 have gone above and beyond their responsibilities and call of duty, risking their own lives to ensure the safety, protection and well-being of children and young people and their families as well as adults who access services.

However, notwithstanding social work and social care practitioners' dedication and heroic actions during the pandemic, as local authorities moved most of their work, practice and services online to ensure continuity of practice and services during the pandemic, this also underlined the gaps in digital practice and online safeguarding skills and the need for greater support and training for practitioners. Therefore, this book is dedicated to social workers and social care practitioners and to bridging that gap and supporting practitioners by offering a versatile view of digital practice and stimulating ethical thinking about the use and implications of social media and digital technologies in practice. We hope you enjoy reading it and thank you again for all you do.

Claudia Megele and Peter Buzzi, May 2020

Notes on contributors

Ruth Allen is the CEO of the British Association of Social Workers and was previously the Director of Social Work at South West London and St George's Mental Health NHS Trust.

Sharon Allen was the previous CEO of Skills for Care and is currently the Chief Executive of Arthur Rank Hospice Charity who support people in Cambridgeshire living with a life-limiting illness and those who need end-of-life care.

Peter Buzzi is the Director of Research and Management Consultancy Centre and the Safeguarding Research Centre. He is also the National Research Lead for the Principal Children and Families Social Worker network's national research and practice development project.

Ian Joseph is a lecturer and researcher at the University of East London with interests in research, youth justice and coproduction. Ian has undertaken work in conjunction with Greater London Authority, Met Police, Youth Justice Board, and Wandsworth Prison.

Sherry Malik is the Director of Children's Services at NSPCC and Non-Executive Director of Dimensions UK. Sherry was previously the Director of Children and Adults Services at London Borough of Hounslow.

Claudia Megele is the Assistant Director of CAFCASS and the National Chair of the Principal Children and Families Social Worker Network. She is also a Fellow of National Institute for Health Research (NIHR) and was previously the Head of Service for Quality Assurance, Practice and Improvement at Hertfordshire County Council.

Lyn Romeo is the Chief Social Worker for Adults. Previously, Lyn worked as the Assistant Director for Adult Social Care in the London Borough of Camden. She has also worked as an inspector with the Social Services Inspectorate.

Naomi Thompson is Senior Lecturer in Youth and Community Work at Goldsmiths, University of London. She was previously a Research Fellow at the Middlesex University and lecturer at YMCA George Williams College.

1

Introduction

Claudia Megele and Peter Buzzi

It was a Saturday afternoon and Sam had just found the wallet and bag she wanted on offer in the sales. She added both to her basket and was getting her card to pay when she heard her work mobile beep: she'd received a message. She had a strict policy of turning her work mobile off during weekends but realised she had forgotten to do so. While she was typing her PIN, she received another beep for a WhatsApp message; Sam uses WhatsApp to keep in touch with the young people she works with. She was concerned and wondered if she should check the messages. Sam's employer had no written policy about use of WhatsApp or any other social media and she had not seen any specific guidance from her employer about communicating with the young people she supported out of hours, but it went against her own rule of setting clear boundaries around her work and turning her work mobile off during weekends. While these thoughts were going through her head there was yet another beep. It felt strange to receive three messages one after another so Sam decided to check. She was shaken when she realised that those messages were from Jo, a young person she was supporting, telling her that she was going to kill herself. Sam responded immediately, trying to help and contain the difficult emotions Jo was experiencing. Sam was able to engage Jo in conversation and Jo was sectioned later that afternoon. This was a serious crisis and Sam was shaken all weekend. On Monday, in a one-to-one meeting with her manager, she was told that she should not use her work mobile during weekends and when she is not on duty. She was reminded of how her actions could blur professional boundaries and result in professional liability for her and her local authority.

Take a moment to reflect on Sam's experience and consider what you would have done if you found yourself in a similar situation. Would you read the messages? Did Sam do the right thing? How about if you were Sam's manager? How would you have discussed this situation with Sam?

Records from the Health and Care Professionals Council (HCPC) show that the HCPC fitness to practise panel sanctioned a social worker with a three-year caution order (HCPC, September 2017); one of the reasons being that the social worker had texted her service user during weekend (twice on a Sunday and four times on a Saturday). These texts were considered inappropriate not because of their context or content but because they were sent over the weekend. This was in spite of the fact that the social worker's employer did not have a written policy prohibiting such contact; Chapter 8 explores this case in more detail.

These examples highlight the multi-layered and complex nature of online engagement and how the omnipresence of social media and the ease of online communication present new challenges for professional boundaries and expectations. This book explores these and other challenges and opportunities associated with social media and their implications for professional practice, identity and boundaries.

Changing workplace and changing social work skills and capabilities

The last half century has seen the increasing application of information technology (IT) in the workplace and the social work profession is no exception. The introduction of new case management systems has had a major impact on social work practice, while the introduction of email and mobile technologies have allowed for mobile working. Platforms such as Skype, WhatsApp and other instant messaging and video conferencing tools have changed the meaning, significance and expectations of presence and professional relationships alongside new ways of data gathering and information processing and a shift from paper-based to paperless working. These and other technologies have transformed the workplace and the professional expectations of and skills required from social workers and social care practitioners.

In the same manner that social workers are expected to learn and to use case management and other IT systems correctly within their organisations, they are also expected to know about the professional and ethical use of emails, mobile phones, SMS, Skype and other social media apps that they may use in their work or for other personal or professional purposes.

Therefore, this book is aimed at supporting students and practitioners to develop their digital and social media literacy and offers an overview of the risks and implications as well as of the positive application of social media and digital technologies across social work practice and regulation. Examining the serious case reviews and fitness to practice hearings relating to the use of social media or failure to ethically consider online risks and their impact in practice demonstrates the increasing complexity of the challenge and the changing expectations for social workers and social care professionals to be able to evaluate and manage online risks not only in relation to their own online identity and behaviour but also in the context of support and safeguarding of children and young people as well as adults who access services.

Thinking of social work values

From online learning to online gaming and from information sharing to online communities, social media offers unlimited potential and resources for our own development and for improving services and support for people who access our services. Indeed, as this book shows, social media can be a great source of resilience for young people. It can also be highly empowering for adults and other people, and can enhance their social capital, resilience and wellbeing. Most practitioners appreciate the value and importance of the online information and resources available to service users. Access to the internet and the ability to use it to meet one's own information needs should be considered as the basic human right of every individual. However, although most practitioners appreciate the value and importance of online information and resources available to service users, most social work assessments and plans do not consider whether or not the service user has internet access and is able to use online information and resources in a helpful manner for their own needs. This perpetuates digital discrimination and continued digital exclusion of many service users who could otherwise benefit from such access.

Furthermore, we would never think of completing an assessment without carefully considering a child's home and school experiences and environment. We also know that children spend increasing amounts of time online and often their development and wellbeing are more influenced by their online relationships and online activities than by their offline experiences. Yet most social work and social care assessments do not consider children and young people's social media and online experiences in discussion with young people or their parents. This presents a significant gap in practice. Therefore, another objective of this book is to raise practitioners' awareness of online risks and enhance their ability to evaluate and manage online risks not only in relation to their own identity and behaviour but also in the context of support and safeguarding of children and young people as well as adults who access services.

From online games to online learning and from YouTube videos to online communities, social media offer a wealth of resources that can be used to support and safeguard service users more effectively. However, social work and social care assessments and plans don't always consider and utilise these resources in an effective manner. Therefore, another objective of this book is to highlight some of the positive use and application of social media in practice to enhance outcomes and better support people who access services. The recent partnership between the NHS and Amazon Alexa, which enables Alexa to offer official NHS advice, although not free from concerns, one example of social media improving support and services.

In a network society with 24-hour connectivity to the internet, most people increasingly rely on online networks, services and relationships to meet their personal, professional and everyday needs. However, online access and the ability to use social media and digital technologies to meet one's own needs have in themselves become a source of digital discrimination and digital exclusion that compounds the many other injustices faced by many service users. Given social work's mission of empowerment and greater equity and equality in society, it is important that social workers and social care practitioners have a more holistic view of social media and its implications for practice and are able to develop the necessary skills to assess and manage online risks and to utilise social media and online resources to cultivate resilience, enhance outcomes and safeguard healthy development and wellbeing of the children, young people and adults who access their services. For example, the ease of recording and posting images and videos online has changed the significance of such images and of recording itself; indeed, once a way of capturing a moment of one's experience, photos/images and videos are increasingly used as a medium for communication.

Changing landscape: born digital and raised social

Our digital lives begin pre-birth and extend post-death. Research indicates that parents share and post an average of 973 pictures before their child's fifth birthday; that is an average of 195 photos per year (Nominet, 2015) and we all know about the pervasive selfie. This has important implications for self-expression, identity, social norms and a host of other factors including social work and personal and professional relationships.

The ease of recording and posting images and videos online has changed the significance of such images and recordings. Photos, images and videos are increasingly used as a medium for communication, one that etches a digital embodiment of one's identity, thoughts, experiences and emotions online.

From the Children Commissioner's 'Growing up digital' (Children's Commissioner, 2017) to the government's 'Digital by default' (UK Government, 2016) agenda, there is evidence of the importance of digital and social media technologies in society and across lifespan. The government's 'Digital by default' agenda specifically states:

> The tools, techniques, technology and approaches of the internet age give us greater opportunities than ever before to help government so that:
>
> - citizens, businesses and other users have a better, more coherent experience when interacting with government services – one that meets the raised expectations set by the many other (non-government) services and tools they use every day
> - elected governments can make a more immediate impact, delivering on policy goals by providing services and information more quickly, with the intended outcomes for their users – and the ability to change delivery quickly if the policy changes
> - the cost and time to build, change and run government is reduced, saving public money and allowing government to respond faster to socio-economic and political change
> - we improve trust between citizens and state, giving citizens confidence that their personal data is secure and being used in ways they expect, while making government activity more transparent and making publicly-owned, non-personal data available for reuse where appropriate
> - we build secure systems by default, ensuring that we create protection against cyber crime through every stage of our digital transformation.
>
> (UK Government, 2016)

The effect and implications of digital and social media technologies run across and impact every layer of human experience, ranging from social and public spheres to personal and private spheres and from interpersonal (our relationships with others) to intrapersonal (our relationships with ourselves). For example, selfies, livestreaming and other forms of online posting enable us to document and share so much more of ourselves and our everyday experiences, activities, feelings and engagements with the world. At the same time, social analytics and artificial intelligence (AI) increasingly shape what we see and our online exposure and experiences. For example, after searching for a product (such as clothing, shoes, music and so on) or service on Google, Amazon, Apple store, or other websites, the ads in your email and on other websites you are browsing (such as online magazines) will feature the products and services that you were searching for earlier. This is a simple example of how our behaviour is tracked online, influences in turn what information we see and, hence, shapes our exposure and experience.

There are many other ways that online information and behaviour (for example, searches, purchases, likes, social media accounts, and so on) can be linked across different devices, social networks, and media. For example, using the same email address to create a new social media account will link the new account to your online identity, even if you use a pseudonym for the account itself in order to maintain your anonymity.

The changes in the way technology contributes to shaping what we see and our online experience have significant implications for individual identity, boundary and privacy and represent an increasing overlap between private and public, personal and professional as well as self and others.

Human beings are social performers and social media has transformed the meaning of performance and presence. We can think of social presence as a performance created through various expressions that are directed at the maintenance of a particular perspective or image, for example, among peers and wider society (Goffman, 1959). In this sense, social media identities and posts are presentations of self and contribute to shaping our social presence. Studies suggest that audiences compare their appearance to media images (Grabe et al, 2008): we compare the way we see ourselves with the way we appear in images and presentations of self. This results in increasing other-awareness and the need to see (that is, voyeurism) and increasing self-consciousness and the need for visibility and audience (that is, being seen) and is one reason for the greater popularity of social media platforms that offer a highly visual medium (such as Instagram or Snapchat) and the recent surge in all types of livestreaming (BBC, 2018).

Given the significance of digital and social media activities in people's lives, there are a number of technology start-ups that are trying to promote digital life after death. The first such attempt, by Liveson.org which had the motto 'When your heart stops beating, you'll keep tweeting', offered a subscription service for Twitter users to enable their accounts to use the company's artificial intelligence software and continue tweeting even after the person's death. Liveson.org did not attract sufficient subscribers and was discontinued. However, other initiatives, such as Eternime, offer similar services by combining the person's online footprint – made up of everything the individual has ever posted on social media including their comments, online profiles, smartphone pictures and so on – with artificial intelligence to create a digital version of the person. In this sense, digital lives potentially begin pre-birth and extend post-death. In fact, a number of law firms offer digital death and digital inheritance advice and services.

In this sense, today's children are born digital and raised 'social' and digital and social media technologies form an integral part of their lives and identities. The impact of technology for adults and older people is no less. From Google search to social networking sites (SNS), from news to online shopping, from online music, games, movies and other entertainments to online learning, e-health, virtual reality and other online goods, services, information and immersive experiences and opportunities, digital and social media technologies are deeply embedded in most people's lives and influence our thinking, feelings, behaviours, and decision making in ways that are not always apparent.

There are many other ways that online information and behaviour (for example searches, purchases, likes, social media accounts, and so on) can be linked across different devices, social networks, and media. Indeed, our everyday experiences are increasingly mediated by social technologies, machine learning and artificial intelligence (AI).

The embedded nature of technology

As social technologies, both in terms of devices (for example, laptops, tablets, smartphones) and media and services (for example, Google, Windows 10, Facebook, Twitter, Instagram, blogs, Skype, email) become increasingly embedded as part of people's everyday lives and experiences, they change the way we relate to technology and through technology to our environment and society as well as ourselves and others. This changed relationship with technology goes beyond the use of digital towards a seamless merging of human and technology and an interweaving of technology in human thinking, relationships and society that offer unlimited new opportunities. For example, we use Google as an extension of our mind and knowledgebase to search for a variety of information ranging from finding an address or the meaning of an unfamiliar word or concept to searching information about products, people, services, events or places, and so on. Indeed, 'our tools are not just external props and aids … they are deep and integral parts of the problem-solving systems we now identify as human intelligence' (Clark, 2004). This merging of human and technology is what Donna Haraway (1984) referred to as cyborg identity.

The embedding of technology in everyday life is not without consequence. On the contrary, these changes have transformed every aspect of life from communication to privacy, friendships, trust, intimacy and relationships, health, education, personal and professional development, life opportunities and life outcomes. For example, social technologies are constructed based on the paradigm of sharing, so online posts and information are 'social' and shared by default; therefore, the onus for ensuring privacy rests with the user of technology. This is a particularly important challenge for social work, social care, health and other relationship-based professions in which privacy and confidentiality of information are central to practice and public trust.

There are a host of other challenges. For example, being born digital, raised social and immersed in digital and social technologies may result in an uncritical acceptance of technology which takes for granted a status of 'social by default' (Buzzi and Megele, 2011; Megele, 2014). This can in turn lead to a 'transparency problem' which can make it difficult for young people to see and recognise the ways in which technology and media influence and shape the world and their perceptions of the world. For example, have you ever seen a child trying to swipe the pages of a print magazine? This is a reflection of how the child thinks about the act of turning the page and of how the experience of digital supersedes and is superimposed onto the experience of physical (Buzzi and Megele, 2011).

Changing practice: risks, opportunities and expectations

In spite of such challenges, non-participation and refusal to engage with social media and digital technologies will only limit the person's own knowledge, resources, opportunities, life choices and possibilities, as well as their outcomes. The rapid changes in technology influence society and our thinking, expectations and understanding of acceptable and unacceptable behaviours and good practice, giving rise to new risks and opportunities. An example of the changing practice expectation is evidenced in Justice Holman's decision to reschedule an adoption hearing, stating:

> So I do wish to highlight by this short judgment that, in the modern era, Facebook may well be a route to somebody such as a birth parent whose whereabouts are unknown and who requires to be served with notice of adoption proceedings. (Holman, 2017)

This acknowledges the need for appropriate and ethical use of social media to support and complement social work and social care practice, but it also raises a number of important questions and ethical challenges relating to the use of social media. Some of these challenges were acknowledged in Justice McFarlane's speech, which highlighted that '… the erosion in the hitherto impermeable seal around the adoptive placement created by social media' requires a new approach and mindset and remains one of the most important challenges for adoption and fostering in the 21st century (McFarlane, 2017).

Social work, however, has had a 'troublesome' (Meyer and Land, 2003, p 1) and uneasy relationship with technology and, in spite of social workers holding and leading in case responsibility, the profession and its leadership role have been undermined by the lack of leadership in technology, digital innovation and related research and theory. However, given the fast-changing practice landscape, it is increasingly evident and essential that social work and social care consider the implications of digital and social media technologies and their impact in practice.

Digital citizenship and digital inequality

Digital citizenship is central to empowerment and equality in contemporary digital and network society (Castells, 2010). Digital citizenship goes beyond digital access and includes digital enablement (that is, connecting individuals to online resources and communities that can either meet their needs or support them in meeting their need), digital rights and responsibilities, and digital safety, security and wellbeing. Digital citizenship also refers to the ability to make appropriate use of technology and its affordances (that is, what it offers) to make safe, responsible, respectful and purposeful choices online to meet one's own needs, develop one's self and enhance one's social capital. Digital citizenship and digital enablement are essential for empowerment and equal opportunities in a digital society.

However, notwithstanding the importance of the UK government's 'Digital by default' (UK Government, 2016) agenda, internet access and digital citizenship are sources of new and increasingly important inequality in society. The Office of National Statistics (ONS, 2017) shows that virtually all adults (99%) aged 16–34 had accessed the internet during the three months prior to the national survey while among adults over 75 only 41% had accessed the internet over the same period. In spite of these figures (and although data demonstrates year-on-year improvement), internet access is not a given and is not equal. Indeed, the 99% figure may be misleading: it reflects the fact that the respondent had accessed the internet during the three months prior to answering the ONS (2017) survey, but this does not mean that respondents had 24-hour internet access or that they had mobile or internet access at home. Indeed, the quality, availability and ease of access to the internet vary significantly across the general population in the UK. Furthermore, not all users have the basic knowledge, skills and capabilities to be able to use the information, resources and affordances of the internet to meet their own needs effectively; this exacerbates individual circumstances and existing inequalities in society.

Given social work's objective of empowerment and greater equality in society, it is important that social work and social care assessments consider service users' access and digital enablement. Furthermore, it is important that all individuals are provided the access, support and training required to enable them to use digital and social media resources in a positive and purposeful manner in order to meet their own needs. Such an approach goes beyond digital literacy and instead promotes digital citizenship and people's holistic identity and well-being both online and offline (Megele with Buzzi, 2017).

A digital journey

This book draws on the knowledge and practice wisdom of a number of national leaders in social work and social care professions in the UK to offer a digital journey that provides an overview of some of the changes, challenges, opportunities and the impact of social media and digital technologies in social work practice and education.

In Chapter 2, Claudia Megele and Peter Buzzi begin this digital journey by examining the ethical implications of social media and the concept of 'e-professionalism'/digital professionalism. The chapter begins by unpacking one of the HCPC fitness to practise hearings and highlights the learning from this case. It then defines and explores the concept of digital professionalism, or 'e-professionalism', followed by a discussion of digital footprints and the blurring of personal and professional boundaries, with another example from the HCPC fitness to practise hearings. This is followed by the introduction of the domains of information sharing and the 'Social Media Activity and Reflection Tool' (SMART) for reflectively mapping and visualising individual's and organisations' social media presence, activities and engagement and for thinking about its implications and ramifications. Chapter 2 concludes with an overview of the digital knowledge, skills and capabilities required for digital professionalism and provides a template for creating an online presence and a social media strategy that promotes digital professionalism.

In Chapter 3, Claudia Megele and Sherry Malik examine the impact of digital and social media technologies in social work when working with children and families. This chapter begins by considering children's use of social media, followed by examining the importance of play and its implications in the context of social media. This leads to a discussion of social media as a developmental space and its impact on children, followed by discussion of a number of challenges and risks in relation to children's use of social media and social work practice including: dark play, #BabyRP, Sexting, cyberbullying, finding and communicating with parents, and online grooming. Megele and Malik conclude by considering some of the salient points in relation to social work and social media in the context of working with children and young people and their parents and carers.

In Chapter 4, Peter Buzzi and Sharon Allen consider the impact of social media for adult social work and social care practice and education. They begin by examining adults' use of social media and the perception of digital competency in practice. They then examine the 'social' in health and social care and consider the implications of social media for relationships and social capital. This is followed by a reflection on the use and application of social media and storytelling for supporting people who access services and as a tool for diversity and advocacy and as an empowering and person-centred alternative for both people with disabilities and people with autism who may prefer alternative modes of communication and self-expression. They then offer an example of a service user's use of social media and examine its implications and ethical challenges. Chapter 4 concludes with some helpful suggestions in relation to the use and applications of social media in social work with adults.

In Chapter 5, Ruth Allen and Peter Buzzi discuss the impact of social media and its implications for mental health social work. Thinking of social media as the new social and emotional environment, they begin by considering the opportunities of social media and networked society for mental health social work and proceed to consider e-interventions and tele-interventions, followed by a discussion of mental health apps and avatar therapy. They highlight the unequal access to services and how social media may be exacerbating inequalities in society, then consider some of the challenges of mental health practice and safeguarding mental health service users online. Highlighting the power of social media for collaboration and coproduction in mental health social work, they conclude with a number of helpful suggestions in relation to the use of social media by mental health social workers.

In Chapter 6, Naomi Thompson and Ian Joseph provide a discussion of social media and youth justice and consider how young people may use social media to evade authority. They invite practitioners to consider a more restorative approach to practice. This is followed by an example of the use of social media to engage young people in an online consultation. They conclude by emphasising the need for more effective use of social media in youth justice and for developing youth justice practice around social media.

In Chapter 7, Claudia Megele and Peter Buzzi offer a reflection and critical examination of online communities and the potential of social media for digital professionalism through the development of and engagement with communities of practice and communities of interest. They begin with a case example involving @SWSCmedia community and draw on this example to demonstrate the dynamics and characteristics of online communities of practice/interest. This includes a discussion of multilogue conversations in online communities followed by a discussion locating @SWSCmedia on the continuum between networks and communities. They go on to examine the relationship between communities of practice and professional identity and concludes by providing some recommendations in relation to creating, developing and facilitating communities of practice.

In Chapter 8, Claudia Megele, Lyn Romeo and Peter Buzzi examine the implications of social media for professionalism and social work regulation. This chapter brings the book full circle as the authors begin with a brief introduction and consideration of the British Association of Social Work's (BASW) social media policy. The chapter then draws on the definition of digital professionalism from Chapter 2 to examine some of the challenges and ethical considerations of social media for social work regulation. The chapter reflects on the case of Peter Connelly and examines whether and when practitioners and local authorities may search, access, view and use service users' social media posts to inform their practice, assessments and planning. The chapter highlights the need for practitioners to be able to identity and assess online/digital risks and to support, advise and safeguard people who access services. They then draw on the HCPC hearing case example from Chapter 2 to underline the implications of this case for regulatory oversight. They highlight the need for regulatory clarity and ensuring that fitness to practise hearings go beyond individual actions and consider the context of any alleged breaches or violations and their wider implications. This is followed by a further example from the HCPC fitness to practise hearings, to examine the impact of online disinhibition and cocoon effects and to consider the tension between freedom of expression and adherence to professional ethics and boundaries. They conclude with a summary of some of the challenges facing social work regulation and regulators.

The final chapter of the book (Chapter 9) examines the evolution of the web and some of the current trends in social technologies and artificial intelligence and their implications for contemporary and future practice in social work and social care.

The fast-evolving social and technological landscapes have transformed society and the understanding of 'social' and are rapidly redefining the 'work' in 'social work'. These changes offer unlimited opportunity but also pose new and unprecedented risks and challenges for social work and social care. Furthermore, there is the persistent perception and belief that social media is an equalising force and force for social good. However, the history of innovation and social transformations indicates that, although innovations may disrupt and replace existing power relations and hierarchies within the social system, they are usually replaced by new forms of power and new hierarchies governed by those who are able to adapt to and exploit the wave of change. Therefore, as social media and digital technologies disrupt the social and innovatively reshape and redefine new social norms and values and new ethics and boundaries, they also replace the existing hierarchies with new heterarchies (that is, evolving, fluid and even ephemeral hierarchies) that dominate the new social order and define the new ethics and, with that, social and professional expectations. This book offers an overview of some of these transformations and critically reflects on their significance and implications for social work and social care practice and education. The editors are grateful to all the authors and contributors who have shared their knowledge, experience and wisdom with us in this book. We have enjoyed writing and editing this book and hope you enjoy reading it.

References

BBC (2018) 'Instagram used more than Snapchat' by US teens, 23 October, https://www.bbc.co.uk/news/technology-45950635

Buzzi, P. and Megele, C. (2011) 'Cyber-communities and motherhood online: a reflection on transnational adoption', in M. Moravec (ed) *Motherhood Online*, Cambridge: Cambridge University Press.

Castells, M. (2010) *The Rise of the Network Society* (2nd edn), Oxford: Wiley-Blackwell.

Children's Commissioner (2017) *Growing up digital: A report of the growing up digital taskforce*. Available at: https://app-t1pp-cco.azurewebsites.net/wp-content/uploads/2017/06/Growing-Up-Digital-Taskforce-Report-January-2017_0.pdf

Clark, A. (2004) *Natural-Born Cyborgs: Minds, technologies, and the future of human intelligence*. Oxford: Oxford University Press.

Goffman, E. (1959) *The presentation of self in everyday life*, London: Doubleday.

Grabe, S., Ward, L. and Hyde, J. (2008) 'The role of the media in body image concerns among women: a meta-analysis of experimental and correlational studies', *Psychology Bulletin*, Vol 134, No 3, pp 460–76.

Haraway, D. (1984) *A Cyborg Manifesto: Science, technology and socialist-feminism in the late twentieth century*. Minnesota: University of Minnesota Press.

HCPC (2017) 'Guidance on social media' (5 September 2017). Available at: http://www.hcpc-uk.org/publications/brochures/index.asp?id=1394

Holman (2017) Family Court: Justice Holman's decision (14 February 2017). Available at: http://www.bailii.org/ew/cases/EWFC/HCJ/2017/19.html

McFarlane, A. (2017) 'Holding the risk: The balance between child protection and the right to family life'. Available at: https://www.judiciary.gov.uk/wp-content/uploads/2017/03/lecture-by-lj-mcfarlane-20160309.pdf

Megele, C. (2014) 'Theorizing Twitter chat', *Journal of Perspectives in Applied Academic Practice*, 2(2). Available at: https://jpaap.napier.ac.uk/index.php/JPAAP/article/view/106

Megele, C. with Buzzi, P. (2017) *Safeguarding Children and Young People Online*. Bristol: Policy Press.

Meyer, J. and Land, R. (2003) *Threshold Concepts and Troublesome Knowledge: Linkages to ways of thinking and practising within the disciplines, enhancing teaching–learning environments in undergraduate courses project occasional report 4*. Available at: https://www.etl.tla.ed.ac.uk

Nominet (2015) 'Today's children will feature in almost 1,000 online photos by the time they reach age five'. Available at: https://www.nominet.uk/todays-children-will-feature-in-almost-1000-online-photos-by-the-time-they-reach-age-five/

ONS (2017) *Statistical Bulletin: Internet users in the UK: 2017*, Office of National Statistics. Available at: https://www.ons.gov.uk/businessindustryandtrade/itandinternetindustry/bulletins/internetusers/2017

UK Government (2016) *Digital by Default Service Standard*. Available at: https://www.gov.uk/servicemanual/digital-by-default

2

Digital professionalism and social media ethics

Claudia Megele and Peter Buzzi

Introduction

Digital and social media technologies have created new opportunities and ways of communicating, seeing, thinking, living and being. They have transformed our way of thinking about and relating to technology, as well as about ourselves and how we relate to others. Although these changes offer unprecedented opportunities, they are also disruptive: they break with the past and transform existing norms, values and behaviours and therefore entail new and significant risks and pose ethical challenges. These challenges are augmented by the rapid pace of technology, which does not allow the possibility for critical examination and evaluation of its effects and implications.

Therefore, this chapter examines the concept of digital professionalism and some of the ethical challenges associated with online identities and engagement. It begins with a case example from the HCPC fitness to practise hearings and highlights some of its learning to underline the need for digital professionalism. It then defines the concept of digital professionalism and explores some of the differences between online and offline environments and their implications for digital professionalism. This includes a discussion about the domains of information sharing and the Social Media Activity and Reflection Tool (SMART) mapping (Megele and Buzzi, 2018) for visualising and reflecting upon one's digital presence and social media engagement and as a component of one's digital citizenship and digital professionalism. This is followed by an overview of the knowledge, skills and capabilities required for digital professionalism and a template for creating, maintaining and evaluating an online identity and presence. The chapter concludes with some suggestions and a summary of learning.

E-professionalim and ethics

This first case example underlines the need for digital professionalism when using social media. It highlights an HCPC fitness to practise hearing and judgement on a social worker's use of Facebook in relation to a case.

Example: Personal and professional use of Facebook

On the eve of a court hearing for a case that was transferred to her about three weeks earlier, an experienced children and families social worker posted the following message on her Facebook page:

> So here it is ... I'm in Court tomorrow for a case where there is a high level of domestic violence amongst many things. So when I'm cross-examined in evidence do you think the judge might question my zero tolerance to domestic violence when he sees the bruises on arms and legs. So I thought I could pull out my tough mudder head band and T shirt as evidence to the Court. (*Community Care*, 2014)

This post was liked by about 14 people. At the time, she had about 100 friends on her Facebook account and thought that her privacy settings would only enable her friends to see the message (based on the social worker's statement about 30 of her Facebook friends were social workers).

After the court hearing and while sitting in a coffee shop with her manager, the social worker posted another Facebook comment stating:

> Just experienced His Honour Judge give parents a massive rollicking. It was an amazing and extraordinary moment in my career and he complimented my Court evidence – how proud am I … . (*Community Care*, 2014)

The above post was accompanied by a small map, pinpointing the location of the court. It received a number of comments, including one from the social worker's manager, in response to which the social worker posted the following:

> Thanks all me and XX are reflecting on how the solicitor commented on fine nails and shoes appear to be a requirement of our team lol. Anyway of [sic] now to do the mammoth grim task fingers crossed xxx. (*Community Care*, 2014)

The 'mammoth grim task' referred to the removal of the children from the care of their parents, and at the end of the same day the social worker posted the following on her Facebook page:

> So the day is complete. Its [sic] powerful to know that … children's lives have just massively changed for the better and now they are safe and protected from harm and have every hope for the future … . (*Community Care*, 2014)

About a week later, her service manager received a complaint from the mother of the children about the social worker's Facebook posts. The service manager Googled the social worker's name; one of the search results was the social worker's Facebook page, which the service manager could access although he was neither a Facebook friend of the social worker nor able to gain access to other private areas of Facebook. The social worker was informed about the complaint and her contract was reviewed by the local authority and not renewed. Subsequently, the social worker was referred to the HCPC for further investigation. In the meantime, the Facebook posts were picked up by a local newspaper.

The HCPC panel concluded that the social worker's fitness to practise was impaired and decided to '... impose a Conditions of Practice Order and concluded that a period of 12 months was the proportionate length of time. The Order will be subject to a mandatory review shortly before the expiry of the order' (*Community Care*, 2014).

This example highlights the need for e-professionalism or digital professionalism and offers a number of important learnings in relation to the use of social media and appropriate professional boundaries:

- First and foremost the social worker in question was in breach of the code of practice, both in terms of the language used and the case-related information posted online. It is inappropriate to share information about a case, even confidentially among colleagues, with the tone and language used in those posts.
- The social worker was under the impression that her privacy settings were such that her posts were visible only to her Facebook friends, while the Google search by her service manager showed that her posts were public and without restrictions. This highlights the ever-changing and complex nature of privacy, and that online posts may be visible to greater audiences than initially intended by the individual. This also highlights the need for careful attention to privacy settings.
- Privacy settings for social media accounts should be checked regularly, especially when installing a new version of an app or when social media companies upgrade or update their software and/or platform; software and system updates may affect your social media account and its privacy settings, sometimes resetting your privacy setting to the default setting.
- Regardless of privacy settings, social media comments or posts can be shared by people in your network (your connections). This may result in your post becoming accessible to a larger audience than originally intended.
- The HCPC statement indicates: 'The Panel paid close attention to the wording of the paragraph, which referred to putting "at risk the confidentiality of service users", not actually breaching it'. This is an important observation: it

demonstrates that fitness to practise cases go beyond 'acts of commission' and occurrence of actual harm and also consider putting 'at risk' and the 'potential' for breach of professional standards. This should be taken into careful consideration when thinking about online posts and digital and social media engagements and their implications and potential for replication and dissemination.

- The HCPC panel concluded that the social worker's fitness to practise was impaired and decided to '…impose a Conditions of Practice Order and concluded that a period of 12 months was the proportionate length of time. The Order will be subject to a mandatory review shortly before the expiry of the order.' This highlights the point that regulatory sanctions such as a 'Condition of Practice Order' go beyond a 'punitive act' and are expected to serve as learning and rehabilitative measure subject to re-examination and further evaluation at a later stage; in this manner, such measures protect the people who access social work services as well as the social work profession and professionals.

Defining digital professionalism or e-professionalism

The preceding example highlights the importance of e-professionalism/digital professionalism. But what is e-professionalism/digital professionalism? The principles of e-professionalism/digital professionalism represent aspirational, moral and human values that apply both online and offline, although their effective application is influenced by context and may vary significantly depending on whether they are on- or offline. Therefore, e-professionalism/digital professionalism requires professionals to extend and apply the profession's offline/face-to-face ethics and values (Reamer, 2017) in a meaningful and contextually relevant manner in digital contexts (Megele, 2012, 2014b; Megele with Buzzi, 2017b). However, this does not mean that digital professionalism is simply an extension of concepts of traditional professionalism. Digital professionalism also involves the ability to identify and effectively manage new risks and opportunities and to use the affordances of digital and social technologies to enhance practice and its outcomes. Indeed, e-professionalism or digital professionalism can be defined as the intersection of the traditional offline professional ethics, values and principles both in relation to the roles, opportunities, risks and challenges of digital and social media technologies and in the context of the changing and shifting social, cultural and political landscape within which professionals operate and professionalism is achieved (see Figure 2.1) (Megele with Buzzi, 2017b).

Although social work values do not change significantly online versus offline, there are differences in the way professionalism is enacted and displayed online and offline. As McLuhan (1964) suggests 'the medium is the message' and there are significant differences between online and offline environments that influence online communication, behaviour and posting and their interpretation and implications. These differences influence professionalism and professional behaviour and their consequences; hence, it is worth briefly examining some of these differences and their implications.

Figure 2.1: Components of digital professionalism

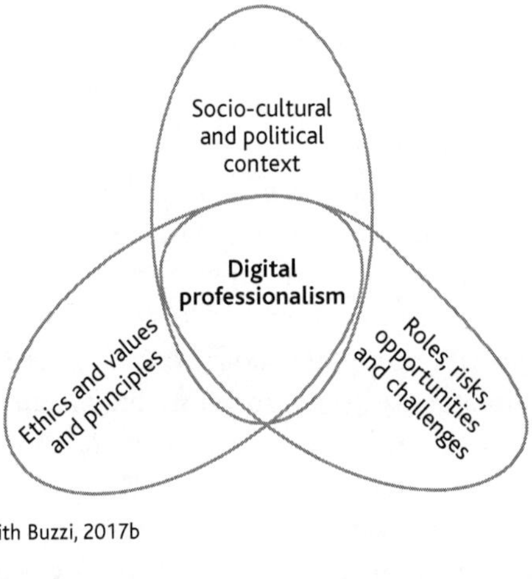

Source: Megele with Buzzi, 2017b

Differences between online and offline communication, posting and behaviours

There are a number of significant differences between online and offline communications, interactions and environments that can influence practitioners' perception of self as well as personal and professional boundaries and behaviour. An understanding of such differences can enhance our understanding and appreciation of the impact of digital and social technologies and the consequences of online communications and posting. Therefore, this section briefly examines some of these differences and their implications for e-professionalism/digital professionalism.

Digital footprint

Online and digital media posts create a digital trace or digital footprint that remains over time and can be searched and retrieved in the future. As a result of this digital footprint, behaviours, communications, interaction and ideas that would have gone unnoticed, undisputed and forgotten in the past find relative permanence online and are often retraceable to the user who posted them.

Every time we interact with digital or social media technologies – be it to check an address, find information, make a phone call, access, view or post on SNS – we add information to our digital footprint and online identity; this includes our use of devices such as smartphones, tablets, computers, and other digital devices, and encompasses software and services ranging from Windows 10, Android software and Google search to Twitter, Facebook, Instagram and Snapchat, and so on. Even when we are not interacting with digital devices and online services, we may be adding information to our online identity; for example, if you have location services activated on your smartphone, your phone and a host of other apps can pick up your location at any time. Furthermore, websites and online services use varying approaches and levels of analysis to gather and generate user data and intelligence. We share a considerable amount of information about ourselves with the world and with different people, organisations and services. Companies such as Apple, Amazon, Facebook, Google, Microsoft, Snapchat and other SNS use this data and multiple other channels and methods to gather increasing user data and deploy artificial intelligence to conduct sophisticated segmentation and analysis of this data and to generate new and valuable intelligence. A large part of this information may not be apparent to the individual. For example, you may not have shared your home address with a given app; however, if that app has access to your location data it can easily work out your home and work address (for example, the most frequent location of your phone overnight is most likely your home address).

The extent of information available about each of us online influences our privacy and poses ethical challenges in relation to personal boundaries, reputation and identity (Reamer, 2013). For example, many employers search applicants' digital footprints to check their backgrounds and evaluate their suitability while the HCPC records demonstrate that regulators may use online posts and digital footprints as evidence in fitness for practice cases. It is important to note that any searches by employers and/or recruiters should be specific and limited to what is important and relevant to the role the applicant is applying for and/or specific criteria relating to that role.

Blurring personal and professional boundaries

The ease of communication through multiple media (for example, text, email, phone, SNS) and flexible anytime/anywhere working and information sharing can blur the boundaries of work and home and personal and professional spheres (van Bochove et al, 2018), and this is further influenced by fluidity of online boundaries. The HCPC fitness to practise hearings (see the case example) demonstrate how different perceptions of appropriate professional behaviour and boundaries can result in misunderstanding and/or grievances and the extent to which regulator may consider sanctions against such breach of professional boundaries.

Example: Professional boundaries and behaviour

The HCPC fitness to practise panel sanctioned a social worker with a caution order (HCPC, 2017) for the period of three years for:

- having texted her service user during weekend (twice on a Sunday and four times on a Saturday). The texts were considered inappropriate not

because of their content but because they were sent over the weekend when her employer offered no social work services; this is in spite of the fact that her employer did not have a written policy prohibiting such contact;
- not having logged the text information in her communication log sheet;
- having disclosed personal information to her service user.

This was in spite of the HCPC acknowledging that a) this was a one-off incident; b) the Registrant had an otherwise 'unblemished record'; c) there was no evidence of actual harm to the service user; and d) there were extenuating circumstances for the Registrant.

Key learning from this case example includes:

- Professional expectations and understanding of what is appropriate can vary significantly between different people; it is important that practitioners are clear and ensure mutual understanding of professional boundaries and expectations with service users.
- It is essential that employers have clear organisational policies and appropriate training and support in relation to expectations, professional boundaries and relationship and communication with service users.

Social by default and merging of private and public audiences

In the past, the separation of audiences enabled professionals to separate their personal and private lives (for example, family activities) from their professional and work life (colleagues and peers). However, the absence of physical boundaries online and the social nature of information result in increasing overlap and merging of private and public audiences online (Fang et al, 2014). Indeed, a distinctive feature of social media is the ease of access to and sharing of online posts and information. Online posts are social and public by default, which means that by default they are open and accessible to large number of audiences often beyond that originally intended. However, effective use of privacy settings can limit the visibility and accessibility of online posts or information. The social nature of information poses an ethical tension between private and public domains and a significant challenge for professions such as social work and social care that operate based on a paradigm of confidentiality and respect for privacy.

Boundaries between self and others

Technology enables individuals to develop an awareness of the other (that is, awareness of the digital projection of the other) (Short et al, 1976) and online communication generates a feeling of connectedness and being involved with others (that is, co-presence) (Rettie, 2005). However, absence of face-to-face, non-verbal cues combined with blurring of boundaries and dominance of textual communication can alter the perception of interaction and self-boundaries, and this can generate a sensation of being merged with the mind of others online (Suler, 2004). In the same manner that when reading a text most people hear the text in their head, reading others' messages can be experienced as a voice inside one's head, generating a psychological presence for the other as if that other was assimilated or introjected into the self and had become part of one's psyche. This can not only alter perceptions of self-boundary and interpersonal dynamics, it can also influence the sense of proximity, intimacy and relationships (Suler, 2004; Megele, 2014b; Megele, 2018; Buzzi, 2020).

Even if one doesn't know the other (for example, their voice or face, and so on), consciously or unconsciously, in one's mind a voice, face and physical appearance – and even thoughts, attitudes and behaviour or behavioural patterns – can be assigned to them. This altered perception blurs the boundary between self and others and is the essence of what Suler (2004) describes as 'solipsistic introjection'.

Digilanguage

The absence of non-verbal communication which accompanies offline face-to-face interactions is replaced by a complex mix of the social presence (Rettie, 2005, 2008) and behavioural cues, influenced by a number of other factors that shape the equivalent of offline non-verbal language online. This non-verbalised, online 'digilanguage' is explained more fully in Buzzi and Megele (2020). For brevity, below is an example of digilanguage and its influence in online communication.

Example: The influence of 'digilanguage'

Imagine you send a private message on Skype to a friend asking her if she wants to go for a drink after work next Thursday. Skype allows you to see when she is typing a message in response and when she is deleting what she has typed. Consider the following scenarios:

Scenario 1: She immediately responds and answers your message saying, 'Great idea. Where'd you like to go?', accompanied with smiley and thumbs up emojis.

Scenario 2: She is typing a response and stops after about 15 seconds but you don't receive any response.

Scenario 3: She is typing a response and stops after about 15 seconds and deletes her message. You can see she is typing again and stops after about 10 or 20 seconds but you don't receive any message.

Scenario 4: She is typing a response to your message and stops after about 15 seconds and deletes her message. She starts typing again and stops after about 10 or 20 seconds but you don't receive any message. The next evening she sends you a message saying 'Ok. Where'd you like to go?'

Each of the scenarios in the overleaf example evokes different thoughts and feelings about your friend and the communication between you. These are the online equivalent of non-verbal language offline and part of the symbolic and non-verbalised 'digilanguage'. Digilanguage influences our communication, relationships and social presence and can lead to misunderstanding. Digilanguage will evolve as apps and social technologies evolve and offer increasing access and visibility to our private and once unseen, unshared and unobservable behaviours. Therefore, practitioners should be aware of the effect of digilanguage in their communications and relationships.

The domains of information sharing

As mentioned earlier, the social nature of digital and social media technologies have blurred the boundaries and created an increasing overlap between individual and social, personal and professional, and private and public spheres. However, both online and offline, practitioners are required to have a clear understanding and awareness and always maintain appropriate professional boundaries. Such respect for boundaries is also necessary when practitioners access, view, handle or manage data and information and the domains of information sharing help in this regard.

Data or information may be personal or professional and it may be private or public depending on the extent to which data or information are known, available or visible to others or can be accessed by others. However, an important feature of social media is that identities, activities and behaviours are 'social by default', meaning there is often the potential the information may be or may become visible or accessible to audiences beyond what was intended by the person who originally posted or shared that data/information. In this sense, online posts are 'social' and shared by default and the onus for privacy rests with the person making that online post to ensure that appropriate privacy settings are applied to limit its audience as need be. This 'social by default' presents an ethical dilemma for relationship-based professions such as social work that operate on an assumption of respect for privacy and confidentiality of information. Therefore, when accessing, viewing, updating or otherwise using or handling data and information, practitioners should consider the domains of information sharing and how our actions and communications and/or online postings may influence or alter the information and/or its domain of information sharing; Figure 2.2 represents the domains of information sharing.

Figure 2.2: Domains of information sharing

Personal (for example, name or home address)	**Personal and professional** (for example, professional, reference)	**Professional** (for example, name of employer)
Personal and private (for example, family relationships)	**Personal and professional and private and public**	**Professional and public** (for example, officers of an LA)
Private (for example, medical records)	**Private and public** (for example, private SNS posts)	**Public** (for example, an open tweet)

Source: Megele, 2018

Although at times the terms 'personal' and 'private' are used interchangeably, they are not the same thing. Specifically, 'personal' and 'professional' are defined based on the nature of information and pertains to information or data sets about a given individual or a group of individuals – in other words it is a *characteristic* of the data set or the information itself – while private and public run on a continuum and are a question of the *extent or degree* of visibility and/or accessibility of the information or data set. Most information or data can be defined by a combination of these (for example, personal and private or professional and public). For example, your health record includes information that is private and personal and that is shared in the professional domain with your GP or the NHS.

Although practitioners should be always mindful in their practice and when handling or sharing information online or offline, particular attention is needed when dealing with information that lies within two or more overlapping domains or when sharing of information moves that information from one domain to another; for example, sharing personal or private information in the professional or public domain.

In social work, for example, notwithstanding the importance of interagency checks in supporting children and families – and although such information may be held by other professionals and agencies and therefore, may already be in professional domain – given that such information is also private and/or personal, the practitioner will need the parent's consent before accessing such information (except in child protection cases).

As a general rule, accessing, viewing, gathering or otherwise handling or processing data that involves private information has ethical implications and may infringe on people's right to privacy. Such situations pose particular ethical challenges. For example, in the HCPC case example at the beginning of this chapter, the social worker shared information that was in private and personal and professional domains in a public domain; it was this repositioning of information in the public domain that resulted in confidentiality risk and the eventual sanction by the HCPC.

To understand the internet and the way people relate to digital and social media technologies Prensky (2001) coined the notion of 'digital natives', referring to those who were born and raised with digital technologies, and 'digital immigrants', referring to those who were born and raised before that period. Although this classification has been used in various research and publications, these are contested terms (Selwyn, 2009) as they label individuals and construct a digital divide between young people and older adults, treating each category as monolithic group; that is, these terms depict young people as technologically equipped, adept and tech-savvy with older people somehow lacking the adeptness of younger people. However, although there are important differences in extent, motivation and quality of online engagement between younger and older people (for example, see ONS, 2017), there are vast differences in each group and their digital and social media knowledge, competence, motivation, confidence and adeptness. Therefore, it is important that practitioners avoid the use of such terms.

In 2011, David White and Alison Le Cornu (2011) used the metaphor of 'tool' and 'space/place' to define the alternative notion of 'residents' and 'visitors' as a way of thinking about the internet and people's online engagements. They state that visitors think of the internet simply as 'one of many tools they can use to achieve certain goals' and not as a 'place' and suggest that this type of social media presence and engagement does not leave any social trace, while residents 'see the Web as a place, ... in which there are clusters of friends and colleagues ... with whom they can share information about their life and work. ... When Residents log off, an aspect of their persona [digital footprint] remains.'

This approach has been used by some social work academics with social work students to think about their social media presence and activities. However, although the concept of digital visitors and residents is a significant improvement on Prensky's idea, this approach presents its own limitations and challenges. Although White and Le Cornu's (2011) notion of digital visitors and residents avoids the categorisation of social media users and their activities by age, the notion of visitor and residents are still in reference to the individual rather than the data or information. Furthermore, considering changes in technology and the 24-hour connectivity and the interactive nature of digital technologies and considering the blurring of online boundaries between private and public and between self and others combined with the complexities of digilanguage, it is difficult to think of social media technologies as a tool that can be used when needed and then filed away without leaving a digital trace and without influencing one's identity and social presence. The incompatibility of the notion of visitors with the way social technologies operate can lead to misunderstanding and ethical confusion in practice. These and other factors challenge the notion of visitors and residents and limit its applicability.

Social media mapping for digital professionalism

Therefore, drawing on the concept of domains of information sharing and focusing on individuals' online posts and activities rather than the way they think about or categorise themselves, Megele and Buzzi (2017a) developed the Social Media Activity and Reflection Tool (SMART) for mapping one's digital presence and social media activities (see Figure 2.3).

Like the work of White and Le Cornu (2011), SMART mapping offers an opportunity to visualise and think about the purpose, type and nature of one's digital and social media engagement and content and whether it is for personal or professional purposes. However, unlike White's approach, this model does not use any metaphors that can add further complexity or label the social media user and instead focuses on the audience, visibility and accessibility of information and social media activities, in other words, the extent to which one's information or social media activity is private or public. Given the importance of privacy and confidentiality of information in practice, this approach is directly relevant to practitioners' experiences and everyday activities.

SMART mapping offers an opportunity to visualise and reflect upon the purpose, type and nature of one's digital and social media engagement and content and whether it is personal or professional in relation to its visibility, accessibility and the extent to which that engagement or content is private or public.

Furthermore, SMART mapping can also represent the relative amount of time spent on each social media app or SNS. Additionally, using colour coding, SMART mapping presents the individual's overall assessment of risks and benefits associated with each social media platform. Figure 2.3 describes the SMART mapping framework while Figure 2.4 offers an example of one practitioner's (Sarah's) SMART mapping.

Megele and Buzzi (2017a) have also developed a motivational language and approach for the use of SMART mapping and the '10 Cs model' described further on in direct work with children and young people. This offers a non-intrusive and relationship-based approach that allows the practitioner to gain an understanding of the young person's motivation and how they use social media as well as their views about online risks, benefits and privacy. Such approaches promote shared understanding, build trust and relationships and ensure better informed and systemic assessment of risks and more effective and holistic safeguarding of young people and adult service users both online and offline.

Here is an outline of how to create a SMART mapping chart:

Figure 2.3: Social Media and Activity Reflection Tool (SMART)

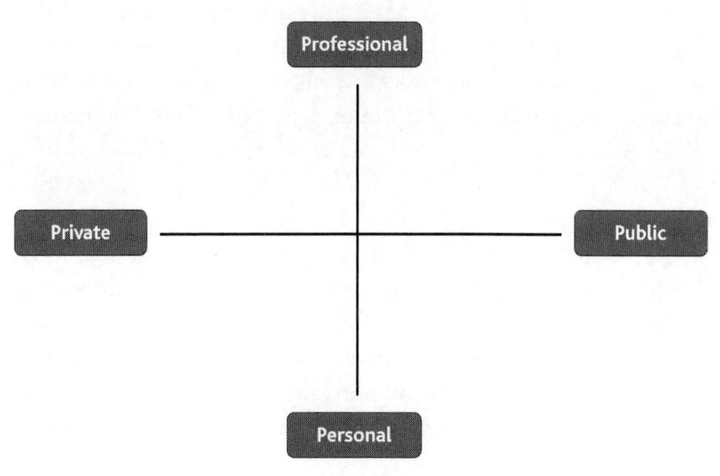

Source: Megele, 2018

- As shown in Figure 2.3, the vertical axis represents the nature of digital engagement and the extent to which it is personal versus professional); the more personal the engagement the closer to the bottom is its mapping while purely professional engagements with no personal aspect are mapped higher up and closer to the top of the page, and data/information that is both personal and professional is placed so that it crosses the horizontal line/axis (see Figure 2.4).

- The horizontal axis represents the audience which is defined based on potential visibility of and access to the online activity, engagement and/or content; audience and visibility and access depend on the privacy settings for a given social media account, or data or content. The more limited the audience, visibility and accessibility of the online activity or content and the more private the posting for a given social media platform the farther to the left is its mapping, while social media platforms and content that are open and visible and accessible to everyone without any restriction are placed further to the right of the mapping. For example, a Facebook page that is only visible to the account holder is placed at the extreme left-hand side of the mapping instead of a Facebook page that is public and open to everyone for viewing and posting of content without any restrictions is placed at the extreme right-hand side of the mapping, while Facebook pages with different privacy settings are mapped in between these two extremes and depend on their level of privacy versus visibility.

- Locating/positioning of social media platforms on the horizontal axis of private and public is based on visibility and therefore, following the Facebook example above, if a Facebook user has a page that is totally private and a page that is totally public the Facebook mapping could be represented by two separate shapes, one toward the right-hand side and the other toward the left-hand side of the mapping or page.

- As shown in Figure 2.4, each digital activity or digital account and each social media app/platform can be shown as a separate rectangle, circle or other shapes, with the relative size of the shape representing the relative amount of time that the user uses that medium or platform; the more time you spend on a given social media platform the bigger the shape representing it.

- As described earlier, the position of a given social media platform on a SMART mapping chart reflects the extent to which it is used for personal or professional purposes versus the extent to which its content is private or public. Hence, if a social media account such as Skype is used for both personal and professional purposes then it can be represented with a shape that crosses the horizontal axis and extends into both personal and professional quadrants depending on the extent to which it is used for personal or professional purposes; for example, if Skype is 70% used for professional purposes and 30% for personal purposes then 70% of the Skype mapping would be above the horizontal line and 30% below the horizontal line (see Figure 2.4).

- The SMART mapping chart can then be used to reflect upon the overall benefits and risks for the individual, using the ROAG colour coding to rate and colour code the overall risks associated with each social media platform (see Megele and Buzzi, 2017a for evaluating online risks):

Red	Very high risk
Orange	High risk
Amber	Medium risk
Green	Low/minimal risk

- Practitioners can then use the mapping to explore and understand a person's social media presence and engagement and explore the person's perspective in relation to a host of important issues including: the person's preference for a given media and the reason for the person's preference; the amount of time spent on a given platform; the person's understanding of online risks in general and the risks and benefits associated with a given platform in light of their activity in particular (here the focus should be on increasing the benefits while mitigating the risks for the person); the person's understanding of the implications and impact of their pattern of digital and social media use on their privacy, identity, relationships, wellbeing and development. This information can be added in bullet point format to complement SMART mapping.

Putting SMART mapping into perspective: social presence

Technology enables individuals to develop an awareness of the other (that is, awareness of the digital projection of the other) (Short et al, 1976) and online communication generates a feeling of connectedness and being involved with others (that is, co-presence) (Rettie, 2005). Therefore, drawing on Goffman's (1959) work on presentation of self, Short et al (1976) were the first to define the social presence theory (SPT) and the construct of 'social presence', defined as 'the degree of salience of the other person in the interaction and the consequent salience of the interpersonal relationships' (Short et al (1976:65). Subsequently Gunawardena (1995) redefined social presence as 'the degree to which a person is perceived as a "real person" in mediated communication'.

Social presence runs on a continuum and, therefore, social presence can be defined at various levels on a spectrum from having an online digital profile to interpersonal and emotional connection between communicators who are perceived as 'present', 'there' or 'real' (Lowenthal, 2010). Therefore, considering the research and the work of various authors, we can think about and define social presence in four different ways:

- Projected presence or a sense of the other (Rettie, 2005; Short et al, 1976); an online social media profile is an example of projected presence.
- Non-individuated co-presence where one assumes or senses the presence of others without being able to individuate the others; that is, psychologically projected others who are always there or always watching but never individuated through actual interaction or online engagement and/or exchange (Megele, 2014a).
- Parallel co-presence or a sense of being with an other who is individuated through their online interactions or digital footprint but their presence is parallel in the sense that, although both parties may be engaged in online activity and on the same platform or online space, there is no direct interaction between the two. For example, two people may engage in an online debate without being aware of one another's presence in the debate.
- Connected co-presence is when two people are co-present as defined in parallel co-presence and in addition to developing or having a psychological connection with the other (Rettie, 2005). This involves direct interaction with the individuated other(s) and can range from chatting with a complete stranger online to continuous connected co-presence where there is a strong social bond and a deep sense of connection and intimacy.

Understanding the level and implications of social presence and digilanguage and their relationship with and impact for the audience, intimacy, privacy and other aspects of one's experience and identity sets the foundation for understanding the ethical and practical implications of online engagements in practice. SMART mapping allows reflection, exploration and visualisation of the person's social presence, online activities and identity and their implications.

Example: SMART mapping Sarah's digital presence and use of social media

Sarah is an agency social worker working in a local authority and uses the following apps:

- Amazon for personal shopping but she has also given feedback for some products she has bought on Amazon, so although her use is mainly personal and private, some part of her activity is in public domain.
- She reads blogs and online news and magazines and actively gives feedback and comments on what she reads.
- She uses Facebook for personal purposes and to keep in touch with her personal friends and family; her posts are visible only to her friends and family.
- Gmail for personal purposes, although she has used her Gmail for communicating with her recruiter and for job applications.
- Office Outlook strictly for professional purposes.
- Google for personal and professional purposes to search addresses and various types of information.
- Skype mostly for professional purposes, with some occasional personal use.
- An anonymous Snapchat account, which is more of a curiosity and which she uses mostly for viewing others' posts although she has also made a few of her own posts.
- Twitter for keeping up to date, connecting with other social workers and engaging in wider social work conversations. She has posted some personal information, for example when having supper with peers or to express personal feelings like having had a busy day and looking forward to a restful evening, and so on.
- Two WhatsApp accounts, one for personal purposes that she uses only with family and close friends and another for professional purposes and to keep in touch with young people.
- Yammer for professional purposes and to exchange information with colleagues within her local authority.

Figure 2.4: Social Media Activity and Reflection Tool (SMART) mapping example

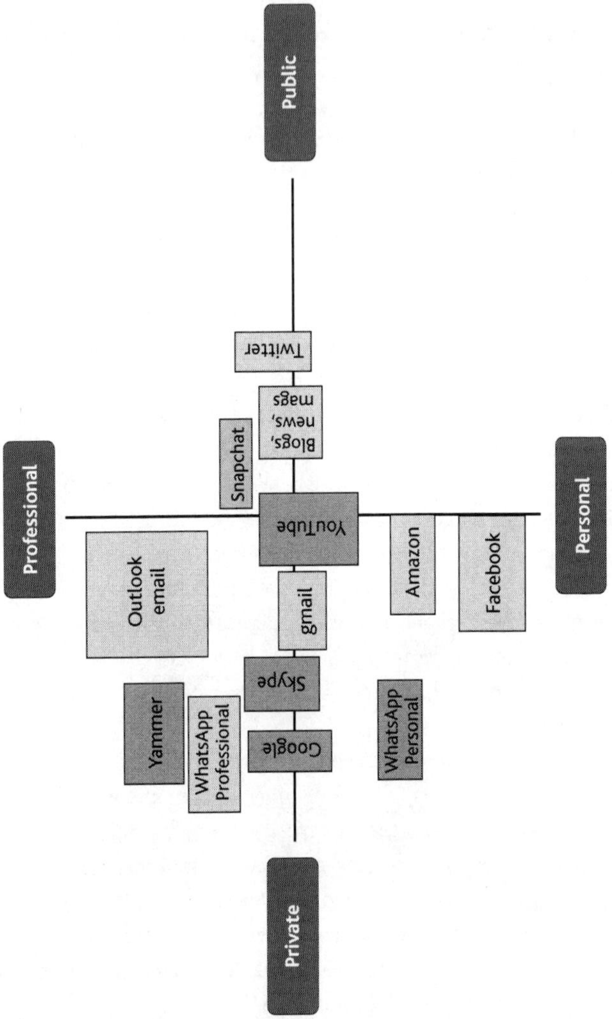

Source: Megele, 2018

- YouTube for viewing videos and movies plus some tutorials for professional purposes. She gives feedback and comments on videos she watches.

Sarah's usage is mapped in Figure 2.4 (note how some of the blocks/shapes extend across different domains of information sharing; for example, the position of Twitter on the mapping represents how much she uses Twitter for personal or professional purposes and whether this information is private or public; in this case her Twitter activity and information are public).

SMART mapping can be used by individuals or at organisational level: for example, practitioners can use SMART mapping to reflect on their own digital and social media presence, activities and engagement. Practitioners can also use SMART mapping as an interactive tool for reflection and working collaboratively with young people and adults to visualise their digital and social media activities and presence and to reflect upon its implications for their privacy and digital identity and its associated risks and opportunities.

Distinctive characteristics of online communication

Online disinhibition effect

People may say or do things online that they would not say or do in offline face-to-face interactions and such difference in behaviour may be due to online disinhibition effect (Suler, 2004). Depending on its extent, online disinhibition can have positive or negative consequences. For example, on the one hand, digital disinhibition can lead to greater self-disclosure, which can be helpful in online therapies and can facilitate online relationships; Suler (2004) refers to this as 'benign disinhibition'. On the other hand, online disinhibition can also result in dissociation from one's online identity and can lead to exaggerated expressions and aggression, including cyberbullying and cyberabuse; Suler (2004) refers to this as 'toxic disinhibition'.

The online disinhibition effect influences social media users to varying extents and depending on a number of different factors. Therefore, practitioners should keep this effect in mind when using social media technologies. The challenge is to keep an open and welcoming approach while ensuring that our online communications, behaviours and engagements are in line with our identity and professional values and ethics.

Dissociative anonymity

Online anonymity refers to the ability to withhold one's identity, for example, by creating online identities and social media accounts with fictitious names or pseudonyms. This allows the individual to project/present an image of their identity that may be similar or quite different from their offline persona, including age, background, personality, physical appearance, gender, lifestyle and lived experiences. This sense of anonymity can enable individuals to a varying degrees to dissociate their self from their online posting and its implications; this can lead to disinhibition and greater self-disclosure.

On the one hand, anonymity may be helpful for young people to explore and experiment with different identities and relationships; on the other hand, it allows them to distance themselves from their online identity, posts and behaviours and can create the feeling that they do not have to own or take responsibility for these. This latter aspect can lead to aggression and transgression of boundaries and different forms of abuse. Online anonymity can reduce self-awareness and result in deindividuation, which can, in turn, lower the person's ability for self-regulation, empathy and perspective taking (Suler, 2004). For example, many sexual offenders, after their capture, admit that the perception of online anonymity gave them a buzz (European Online Grooming Project, 2012).

Practitioners who would like to engage on social media while maintaining their anonymity can use a pseudonym on their social media account. However, regardless of whether their social media accounts are anonymous or named, social workers will still be expected to adhere to social work's professional values and ethics.

Furthermore, it may be helpful to note that social media companies use multiple data points for identifying individuals and linking their account with their activities and/or behaviour. Therefore, an anonymous account can still be retraced to an individual's other social media accounts and online activities in a number of ways. For example, using your personal or professional email to create an anonymous social media account can link the social media account with your profile. In the same manner, using the same device can link two social media identities (for example, using two different social media accounts on the same mobile phone). There are a host of other ways to cross link online accounts and activities to a given profile and therefore, most 'anonymous' accounts may be retraceable to their users and, therefore, are not as 'anonymous' as one may think.

Asynchronocity

Offline face-to-face interactions are interactive and synchronous, that is, take place in real time and therefore, require immediate response. However, most online interactions are asynchronous (that is, they can take place at intervals and over a period of time), hence it is acceptable for one to receive a response to an online post/message after some time; for example, depending on the situation, it may take from several minutes to hours or even days before one receives a reply. This reduces the demand for immediate reaction and allows individuals to think about and formulate their response or reframe the situation and/or their answer; this can augment the online disinhibition effect (Suler, 2004; Megele, 2014a, 2014b) and the individual's behaviour in these cases is part of the new digilanguage described earlier in this chapter.

Invisibility

Most online interactions are text-driven and in most text-driven online environments people cannot see each other; for example, when participating in forums, reading or posting a comment, or other online engagement, they cannot see others in person.

This physical invisibility enhances the effect of dissociative anonymity and can result in greater disinhibition. Indeed, face-to-face, video or audio interactions are more taxing as they require close attention to verbal and non-verbal cues (Burgoon and Dunbar, 2006; Megele, 2014a). However, in text-based communications, users are better able to pace the conversation (have greater reaction time) and can even multitask during the conversation. The text-driven communication's lower emotional and mental demand and present several important advantages. For example, textual communication can be a helpful alternative for communicating with autistic people or people who experience mental health difficulties and others who may experience emotional overload and/or anxiety in face-to-face communication.

Although there is an overlap between invisibility and dissociative anonymity, they are not the same thing; for example, people in an online chat may know a great deal about each other but still cannot see or hear each other, and can experience increased disinhibition due to invisibility. Therefore, invisibility has a compounding effect that magnifies both the perception of anonymity as well as the online disinhibition effect (Suler, 2004; Megele, 2014a; Megele with Buzzi, 2017b).

Minimisation of status and authority

The internet has a levelling effect, in the sense that often one's power, status and authority offline seems to be irrelevant or of little impact online. Potentially this can contribute to greater equality (Suler, 2004) or more accurately a new fluid hierarchy based on a new and changing set of criteria including: the person's online popularity, followers, social network activity, digital knowledge and capabilities, digital and social capital, and so on. This offers opportunities for advocacy and promotion of new and old causes. However, this also means that digital and social media can be instrumentalised and used as a social or political 'weapon' to obscure, damage or distort others' views and digital presence. This can also be used positively; for example, the presence of the police in a neighbourhood can serve as a deterrent to crime, the presence of the police/

authorities online combined with effective digital citizenship can indirectly contribute to reducing incidences of cyberabuse and cyberaggression, including cyberbullying.

The cocoon effect

The cocoon effect is the result of insulating or hiding oneself from one's social environment, which may be perceived as different, distracting, unfriendly, dangerous, or otherwise unwelcome, at least for the present. Technology has made cocooning easier than ever before. Digital devices and online experiences can be highly engaging and can absorb the user in a sort of immersive experience that allows individuals to separate themselves from their surroundings and block out their environment. Social media and digital devices enable people to meet, connect and communicate with others online or join online communities although they may be physically alone or isolated. Social media and digital technologies also enable individuals to tailor their social network and interactions (Groot Kormelink and Costera Meijer, 2014) by choosing who they connect with and the type of content and information they see, interact with and respond to. This can limit one's experience and the diversity of ideas, beliefs, data and information we are exposed to and can result in a distorted and limited vision of the world and limit our choices and possibilities.

Furthermore, social media and most online apps and interactions are increasingly mediated by artificial intelligence and machine learning that examines our every action, interaction and choice online. In particular, social media companies use machine learning to personalise the content we are exposed to based on our previous choices and preferences and this can accentuate the cocoon effect and further narrow our experience.

Connecting only with likeminded individuals and organisations based on one's own ideas, beliefs, preferences and agenda can create an echo chamber for one's thoughts, emotions and ideas, reinforcing one's views and diminishing one's openness and acceptance of difference and diversity and appreciation or respect for others' views. This can create a cocoon effect (Megele with Buzzi, 2017b).

The cocoon effect suggests that individuals' online community and the level and type of their online interactions and engagement influence and structure their perception and evaluation of self and others online and their communications and interactions in that environment.

The cocoon effect can lead to dissociating experiences and can result in negative outcomes. For example, the cocoon effect is evident in everyday experiences and can range from benign experiences where people use digital devices such as phones and headphones to block out their environment and create a preferred parallel experience during their daily commute, to toxic experiences such as extremist or pro-harm communities that serve as an echo chamber promoting dangerous and damaging beliefs, ideas, values and ideologies.

The cocoon effect has been an important contributory factor in a number of cases involving social media and professional misconduct as evidenced in some of the HCPC fitness for practice hearings; Chapter 8 offers a case example of social media and social work regulation that demonstrates the role and impact of the cocoon effect.

Digital professionalism: knowledge, skills and capabilities

The social media policy of the British Association of Social Workers (BASW), first developed in 2012 and then revised in 2018, offers some helpful guidance in relation to social media use by social workers. However, unfortunately these policies do not address some of the more pressing ethical and professional issues in relation to the use of digital and social media technologies in practice facing social workers and social care practitioners. Therefore, the Principal Children and Families Social Worker (PCFSW) network launched a national research and practice development project with specific focus on digital professionalism and online safeguarding to address the gap in literature and guidance in this important and fast developing area of practice.

With over 2,000 social work participants, the PCFSW research project is the first project of its kind that has the depth and breadth to offer an evidence-based understanding of digital practice across the country and produce an evidence-based and systematic approach to assessing online risks and safeguarding children and young people online. This book and this chapter draw on some of the learning from that research.

Given the differences between online and offline communications, interactions and environments and considering the definition of digital professionalism, there are a number of important knowledge areas, skills and capabilities that are required for developing practitioners' digital professionalism and digital citizenship. Indeed, given the importance of adherence to a professional code of ethics at all times, both online and offline, it is worth briefly examining some of the knowledge, skills and capabilities that are needed to support and develop practitioners' digital professionalism.

Figure 2.5 presents an overview of the knowledge and skills required for digital citizenship and digital professionalism; these provide a base for digital citizenship and include learning about:

- **Privacy and digital/online boundaries** and how they are impacted by the medium and context.
- **Digital communication and relationships** across multiple media and different modes of communication and their appropriate and ethical use.
- **Digital footprint** and its implications and impact, and how to establish, manage and maintain an appropriate digital footprint.
- **Self-image and identity** and online identities and the risks, opportunities and implications associated with them.
- **Reputation management** and building upon the affordances of technology (for example, digital footprint, self-image and identity) to manage and enhance one's reputation.
- **Digital and information literacy** and using digital and social media technologies in a relevant, age-appropriate and developmentally appropriate manner.
- **Safety and security** ranging from the use of virus protection and firewalls to parental protection and appropriate online privacy settings, and so on.
- **Online risks, resilience and opportunities and digital safeguarding** going beyond technological safety to consider

digital safeguarding, cyberaggression and cyberabuse (for example, cyberbullying, online grooming and exploitation, digital harm, and so on).

- **Digital ethics and digital citizenship rights and responsibilities** involving knowledge and awareness of one's digital rights and responsibilities and appropriate professional ethics in digital context.
- **Proactive citizenship and understanding the role of the bystander.** Research indicates that most bullying occurs in the presence of bystanders (witnesses) (Nickerson et al, 2014), and the presence of silent bystanders (not to mention those who support and encourage the bully) socially validate the bully and are source of power for the bully (Megele with Buzzi, 2017b). Research has also shown that bystander intervention in favour of the victim has a significant impact on prevention of bullying. Therefore, proactive digital citizenship and understanding the role and responsibility of bystanders has an important impact on mitigating digital harm and improving digital experiences of all concerned and as such is an important aspect of digital ethics and professional digital practice as well as digital professionalism and online safeguarding. This also represents an application of anti-oppressive, anti-discriminatory and empowerment principles in social work.

Figure 2.5: Knowledge and skills for digital citizenship and digital professionalism

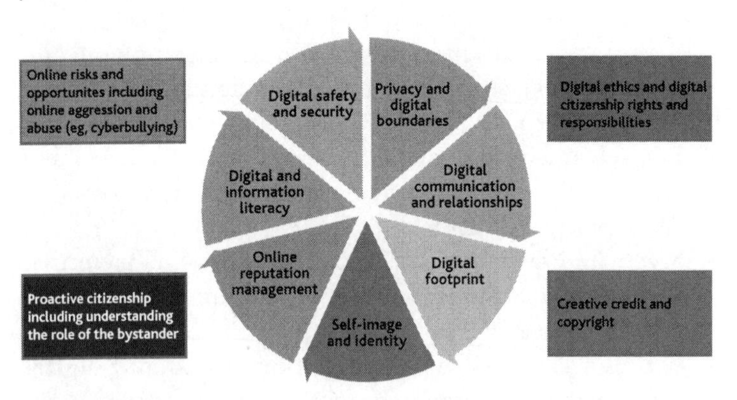

Source: Megele and Buzzi, 2017a

- **Digital and self-identity** and the implications of online communication and behaviour for self-identity.
- **Creative credit and copyright** including production, use and management of user-generated content.

In addition to the listed knowledge and skills, there are a number of digital capabilities that are needed to ensure practitioners are able to use digital and social media technologies in an effective and appropriate manner to support people who access services, develop their professional identity and enhance their practice. Figure 2.6 presents an overview of the following digital capabilities required for digital professionalism:

- **Simulate**: interpret and construct models of the world (for example, problems, solutions, processes). The capability to interpret our experience and create models of the world is essential both online and offline as it facilitates understanding of the world, experiences and events; this is particularly important online given the multitude of possibilities and fluidity of online and virtual experiences and spaces (such as virtual reality).
- **Multitask**: in a fast-paced society multitasking is an essential capability in order to effectively manage the multiple demands of contemporary life. This is much more important in online settings where asynchronous communication result in multilogue rather than dialogue, when multiple voices can speak simultaneously and yet be heard (Megele, 2014a) (for example, through emails or online posts), and with multiple threads of conversation and tasks competing for practitioners' attention. In such an environment, the capability to scan the environment and shift focus onto salient information and details is fundamental for ensuring a timely and professional response, action and engagement.
- **Coproduce**: partnership working has always been an important element of social work professional capabilities and the ease of online information sharing and the social nature of social media offer unprecedented opportunities for doing so. Therefore, it is essential that practitioners use such opportunities to transcend the traditional silos and boundaries

Figure 2.6: Digital capabilities for digital professionalism

Source: Megele, 2018

and collaboratively and productively achieve common goals and coproduce shared solutions and outcomes.

- **Network**: in a networked society the capability to connect, share and relate to others to develop one's social capital in a meaningful manner is indispensable for developing individual's identity and social capital.
- **Enhance capabilities**: use and relate to technology as an extension of self to enhance one's own and others' experience, knowledge, thinking and decision making.
- **Curate**: select, collect, organise and present content and information using professional knowledge and expertise, and evaluate the reliability and credibility of information and sources.
- **Transmedia appropriation**: follow and gather data and information from across multiple sources and media, and remix media and content to produce meaningful information.
- **Negotiate**: negotiate one's journey across diverse communities and media, and recognise and appreciate diversity and difference, and multiple perspectives and diverse values and norms.
- **Pool knowledge and experiences**: pool knowledge and expertise and tap into collective intelligence to inform, complement and enhance one's thinking, knowledge and behaviour.
- **Ethical recognition**: assess varying circumstances and respond in an appropriate, ethical, proportionate and professional manner.
- **Digital citizenship**: identify and manage online risks and opportunities and make respectful, purposeful and meaningful choices.

A template for creating, assessing and maintaining online/digital presence and engagement

Online posts and activities and online relationships and interactions with others are digital projections of our identity; these expressions of identity remain as digital footprints and shape people's online identity and self-narrative. Therefore, the following present the dimensions of online identities and are helpful mindlines/reminders for creating and evaluating or creating and maintaining a coherent online identity and social media presence. (Mindline is a term used by the author to highlight points to keep in mind or mindful reminders.)

Context: What social media platform will you use and what are its characteristics? What are the advantages, limitations, risks and opportunities associated with that social media network or medium? Are there any ethical, personal or professional implications?

Mindline: Each SNS has its own strengths, limitations, risks and opportunities and emphasises a different type of communication and interactions. For example, there are evident and significant differences in content and mode of communication between Twitter, Facebook, Instagram, YouTube and Snapchat.

Compatibility: Decide and define the reason for your social media presence/account, and decide whether you wish to have a named or anonymous account. Are your online identity, engagements and posts in consonance and compatible with your offline identity and experience?

Mindline: As a digital professional it is important that your online identity is in consonance and compatible with your offline identity and professional ethics and values. Dissonance and irreconcilable discrepancies between online and offline identities can result in lack of authenticity and raise ethical questions and professional challenges.

Connection and social capital: Who is your audience and who do you want to connect with and how will you choose who to connect with and who not to connect with? Is there an overlap or conflict between your personal and professional connections/audience? Does this overlap generate any ethical issues or conflict between the two?

Mindline: As a digital professional, the choice of your social network and who you connect to does not only influence your social capital, it can also have important ethical and professional implications. For example, would you accept a friend request from a parent or a young person who is your service user?

Content: What sort of information and content do you wish to share with your network? And what sort of content will you seek, search or be exposed to? Does this raise any ethical, personal or professional questions or issues?

Mindline: Your engagement and content need to be in line with your professional ethics and values and your employment contract and employer's policies.

Confidentiality and personal disclosure: Do you share private and personal information with your network? If yes, what sort of personal or private information will you share? And what sort of personal or private information can be derived from your profile or posting? What are the implications of these and what are the risks and opportunities? Are there any ethical, personal or professional implications?

Mindline: Think about any potential conflict between your personal and professional activities or identities and its potential implications for your professional identity.

Contact: What are the risks of coming in contact with an abuser or source of abuse or online aggression, either directly or indirectly? How will you deal with such a situation?

Mindline: Privacy settings regulate the visibility of online identity and activities and the extent to which different people can comment and interact with your posts and conversations. Therefore, it is helpful to think about possible scenarios and have a clear and thoughtful approach to managing harmful or abusive and aggressive contacts.

Conduct: What is your online conduct/activity (that is, your communication and online engagement)? Is this compatible with professional values and ethics and your employer's policies? Do your social media communication and conduct raise any ethical, personal or professional questions?

Mindline: It is important to note that, regardless of the situation, you are bound by professional ethics and so it is important not to engage in or mirror inappropriate communication or behaviour. Instead, as a digital professional it is important to report any online aggression, abuse or other forms of inappropriate behaviour that you would report in an offline setting.

Consumption: How much time do you dedicate to your social media account and online identity? What is the frequency and pattern of your online engagement? How frequently do you post information and updates and how frequently do you communicate and interact with others? Consistency and coherence in content and updates is an important factor in developing one's online identity and social capital.

Mindline: the pattern and frequency of online activities and social media engagement can be correlated with people's mental state and emotional experience such as anxiety or self-esteem while the time stamp for each post freezes our digital footprint at a point in time. These can reveal significant information about the individual and therefore require thoughtful consideration.

Commercial exploitation: Do you have any professional or commercial objectives? What are the positive and negative professional and commercial potential of your online identity and activity?

Mindline: Online engagement can help you raise your profile and promote your personal or professional values, ideas or your work. Furthermore, a large and well-designed online identity and network can enhance one's social capital and influence and may also generate commercial value.

Conclusion

There are unlimited opportunities offered by digital and social media technologies that can enhance practice and services. However, the social nature of technologies on the one hand facilitates collaboration and coproduction of services while on the other hand posing ethical challenges for privacy, confidentiality and boundaries between personal and professional identities. Therefore, this chapter has defined and examined the importance of digital professionalism or e-professionalism for social work and social care professionals. It has also examined the differences between online and offline communications, behaviours, and posts and presented the domains of information sharing and social media mapping for digital professionalism. It has provided a tool for reflection and for mapping social media use and engagement in relation to digital citizenship and digital professionalism. In addition, it has outlined the knowledge, skills and capabilities required for digital professionalism and offered a template for thinking about, reflecting upon and configuring/shaping one's online identity and presence.

Some of the learning points from this chapter include:

- The increasing use of digital in services underlines the importance of digital professionalism and e-professionalism in practice. This requires the development of the digital professionalism knowledge, skills and capabilities covered in this chapter.
- Social workers have a dual mandate to support and safeguard and promote equality and their digital and social media engagement should be considered within that remit and in relation to their professional standards and employer's policies and guidance.
- Employers can check on practitioners' online behaviour and social media accounts for pre-employment (CIPD, 2013) however, employees should be appropriately advised of such practices.
- Safe working policies should include digital and social media use and employers should have clear guidance in relation to digital safeguarding, digital professionalism and for the use of digital and social media technologies in practice.
- Practitioners should consider that guidance often refers to principles and is non-specific; therefore, it should be considered both online and offline in a contextually relevant manner.
- Care is needed to ensure that communications and interactions do not result in unintentional disclosure that may jeopardise personal or professional boundaries, relationships or information.

- Practitioners should ensure that their digital and social media activities are in line with their employment contract, employer's policies, and professional regulation and guidance.
- Practitioners' online behaviours, posting and interactions should not undermine their employer and/or create potential liability for anyone.
- In general, professionals should interact in such a way that their actions and communications can stand public scrutiny.
- Although accounts may be private, your social media posts can be reposted onto the open web.
- As a general rule, practitioners should avoid using personal accounts or personal devices for professional purposes. For example, practitioners should not use a personal phone to take photos for professional purposes or personal social media accounts (for example, a personal Facebook account) to communicate with service users or their families and carers.
- For establishing a meaningful social media presence, practitioners need commitment to an online presence, continuity of engagement, and consistency of message.
- Ethics and professional conduct are defined by people, society, culture and context. Therefore, given the rapidly evolving professional, social and cultural landscape, the professional expectations and ethics and standards of appropriate professional behaviour are also changing apace, and that means at times the interaction may define the rule and practice may precede policy and interaction may define the rule.

References

Burgoon, J. and Dunbar, N. (2006) 'Nonverbal expressions of dominance and power in human relationships', in V. Manusov and M.L. Patterson (eds) *The SAGE Handbook of Nonverbal Communication*, London: Sage, pp 279–98.

Buzzi, P. (2020) *Relationship-based Practice in Digital Age*. London: PSW Network.

Buzzi, P. and Megele, C. (2020) 'Digilanguage: The new non-verbal online language and its components and interpretation'. London: PSW Network.

CIPD (2013) 'Pre-employment checks: An employer's guide'. Available at: https://www.cipd.co.uk/knowledge/fundamentals/emp-law/recruitment/pre-employment-checks-guide

Community Care (2014) 'HCPC sanctions social worker over Facebook posts'. Available at: http://www.communitycare.co.uk/2014/09/10/social-worker-given-conditions-practice-order-disrespectful-facebook-posts/

European Online Grooming Project (2012) *Final Report*. Available at: http://natcen.ac.uk/media/22514/european-online-groomingprojectfinalreport.pdf

Fang, L., Mishna, F., Zhang, V. F., Van Wert, M., and Bogo, M. (2014) 'Social media and social work education: understanding and dealing with the new digital world', *Social Work in Health Care*, 53(9): 800–14.

HCPC (2017) 'Guidance on social media' (5 September 2017). Available at: http://www.hcpc-uk.org/publications/brochures/index.asp?id=1394

Goffman, E. (1959) *The Presentation of Self in Everyday Life*, London: Doubleday.

Groot Kormelink, T. and Costera Meijer, I. (2014) 'Tailor-made news: meeting the demands of news users on mobile and social media', *Journalism Studies*, 15(5): 632–41.

Gunawardena, C. (1995) 'Social presence theory and implications for interaction and collaborative learning in computer conferences', *International Journal of Educational Telecommunications*, 1(2): 147–66.

Lowenthal, J. (2010) *Using Mobile Learning: Determinates Impacting Behavioral Intention*. Available at: https://doi.org/10.1080/08923647.2010.519947

McLuhan, M. (1964) *Understanding Media: The Extensions of Man*, Cambridge, MA: MIT Press.

Megele, C. (2012) 'Social care in the e-professionalism era', *The Guardian*. Available at: https://www.theguardian.com/social-care-network/2012/apr/25/eprofessionalism-social-care

Megele, C. (2014a) 'Theorizing Twitter chat', *Journal of Perspectives in Applied Academic Practice*, 2(2). Available at: https://jpaap.napier.ac.uk/index.php/JPAAP/article/view/106

Megele, C. (2014b) 'eABLE: Embedding social media in academic curriculum as a learning and assessment strategy to enhance students learning and e-professionalism', *Innovations in Education and Teaching International*, 52(4): 414–25.

Megele C. (2018) 'Social media, digital professionalism and CPD: Strategic briefing', *Research in Practice*. Available at: https://www.researchinpractice.org.uk/children/publications/2018/december/social-media-digital-professionalism-and-cpd-strategic-briefing-2018/

Megele, C. and Buzzi, P. (2017a) *Digital Professionalism and Online Safeguarding Course*. London: PSW Network.

Megele, C. with Buzzi, P. (2017b) *Safeguarding Children and Young People Online*. Bristol: Policy Press.

Megele, C. and Buzzi, P. (2018) *Digital Professionalism in Social Work and Social Care*. Presentation and workshop. London: PCFSW Network.

Nickerson, A., Aloe, A., Livingston, J. and Feeley, T.H. (2014) 'Measurement of the bystander intervention model for bullying and sexual harassment', *Journal of Adolescence*, 37: 391–400.

ONS (2017) *Internet Users in the UK: 2017*. Office of National Statistics. Available at: https://www.ons.gov.uk/businessindustryandtrade/itandinternetindustry/bulletins/internetusers/2017

Prensky, M. (2001) 'Digital natives, digital immigrants', *On the Horizon*, 9: 1–6.

Reamer, F. (2013) 'The digital and electronic revolution in social work: Rethinking the meaning of ethical practice', *Ethics and Social Welfare*, 7(1): 2–19.

Reamer, F. (2017) 'Evolving ethical standards in the digital age', *Australian Social Work*, 70(2): 148–59.

Rettie, R. M. (2005) 'Presence and embodiment in mobile phone communication', *Psychology Journal*, 3(1): 16–34.

Rettie R. (2008) 'Connectedness, awareness and social presence'. Available at: https://www.researchgate.net/publication/38175268_Connectedness_Awareness_and_Social_Presence

Selwyn, N. (2009) 'The digital native: Myth and reality', *Aslib Proceedings*, 61: 364–79.

Short, J., Williams, E. and Christie, B. (1976) *The Social Psychology of Telecommunications*, London: Wiley.

Suler, J. (2004) 'The online disinhibition effect', *Cyberpsychology and Behaviour*, 7(3): 321–6.

Van Bochove, M., Tonkens, E., Verplanke, L. and Roggeveen, S. (2018) 'Reconstructing the professional domain: Boundary work of professionals and volunteers in the context of social service reform', *Current Sociology*, 66(3): 392–411. Available at: http://journals.sagepub.com/doi/abs/10.1177/0011392116677300#articleCitationDownloadContainer

White, D. and Le Cornu, A. (2011) 'Visitors and residents: A new typology for online engagement', *First Monday*, 16(9).

3

Social media and social work with children and young people and looked after children

Claudia Megele and Sherry Malik

Introduction

Take a moment to consider how children think about, assess and relate to technology and how that may differ from adults thinking about technology. While many of us who work with children did not grow up with contemporary digital and social media technologies, most of the young people we work with cannot imagine a world without it, and while some adults may still consider digital and social media of little importance or unhelpful, distracting or even dangerous, these technologies are an integral part of young people's lives and identities (Megele with Buzzi, 2017a). Such technologies have become embedded in everyday life and have transformed human thought and consciousness and even notions of time, place, space, boundary, proximity, friendship and relationships, influencing people's everyday choices and behaviours. Indeed, young people move seamlessly between online and offline realms and virtual/online and physical/offline are inseparably intertwined in the fabric of their lives and experiences (boyd, 2007; Livingstone, 2008; Valkenburg and Peter, 2009; Buzzi and Megele, 2011).

Livingstone et al (2011) argue that digital activities can be a great source of learning and empowering for children and young people. The European Commission's Joint Research Centre (Stewart et al, 2013) initiative 'Digital Games for Empowerment and Inclusion' is an example of a project aimed at the effective use of gamification and digital technologies for empowerment of young people.

Therefore, drawing on the concept of 'cyworld' (boyd, 2007) and the work of Livingstone (2008) and Livingstone and Haddon (2009), Megele and Buzzi (2017a) argue that practitioners and organisations should promote children's and young people's digital rights and digital citizenship, and that this requires recognising and appreciating the transformation of human experience and its liminal (simultaneously online and offline) nature and thinking about childhood as 'cyborg childhood' within that context. Megele and Buzzi go on to present a new child-centred and systemic model (the 10 Cs model) for assessing online risks and resilience, and the assessment diamond (Figure 3.1) for holistic safeguarding of children and young people.

This chapter explores some of ways in which digital and social technologies influence children's lives and social work and social care practice. It begins with an overview of children's and young people's use of social media and some its implications. This is followed by a discussion of social media and 'play' and a reflection on social media as a developmental space and considers the importance of social media for young people's relationships and identity. It then examines how digital and social media are leading to new behaviour and generating new forms of risks for children and young people, resulting in new challenges for safeguarding and social work and social care practice. Specifically, this chapter considers examples of 'dark play' and #BabyRP (Baby Role Play), sexting, cyberbullying, children in care and adoption services, and online grooming. In conclusion, it draws on some of the more important points from the chapter to offer some recommendations.

Figure 3.1: Assessment diamond for holistic safeguarding of children and young people

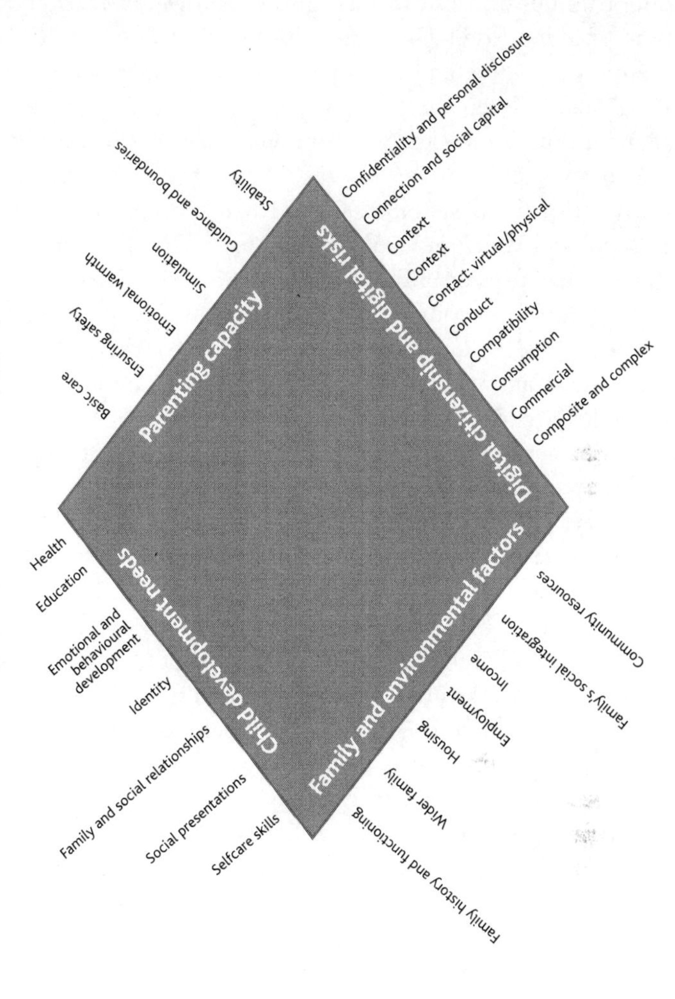

Source: Megele with Buzzi, 2017a

Children's and young people's use of social media

The internet is an exciting and unknown place to explore, and children and young people are naturally curious; this offers unlimited possibilities for learning and creative and productive opportunities that lead to their growth. However, it also poses new and increased risks and challenges, for example, the merging of online and offline as a single seamless experience may make children and young people more prone to meeting a stranger offline once they have known them online (Haraway, 1991; boyd, 2007; Megele with Buzzi, 2017a). A freedom of information request (NSPCC, 2016) to police forces across England and Wales found 5,653 child sex offences that involved the internet in England and Wales in 2016/17. Furthermore, young people can come across inappropriate content, including pornography, by mistake or they may look for it because they're curious or are drawn in by promises by advertisers. Indeed, Barnardos (2019) indicates that 83% of 11-year-olds participating in their research have seen something inappropriate or have communicated with people they don't know online who have asked them to do things they don't want to do. It also indicates that, while three in ten children aged 8–15 who use social media still believe that all or most of what they see on there is true, two-thirds believe that only some of what they see is true. Children were shown an image of a Google search result and were asked why the first four results on the page were there (these were distinguished by a green box with the word 'Ad' in it). Only a quarter of 8–15s gave the correct response, that the results were adverts/paid to be there. This is the same as five years ago (24% in 2015) and shows that children's critical understanding of Google search is the same as five years ago. Furthermore, the Barnardos (2019) report found that 83% of 11-year-olds participating in the research have seen something inappropriate or have communicated with people they don't know online who have asked them to do things they don't want to do. Ofcom (2019) found that half of 12–15s who go online say they had seen something hateful about a group of people in the past 12 months – up from 34% in 2016 – and the majority (58%) chose to ignore it. Overall, 61% of adults and 79% of

12-15-year-old internet users say that they have had at least one potentially harmful experience online in the past 12 months, while 29% of adults and 38% of 12–15-year-old internet users have experienced something that they rated as 'harmful'. These data indicate that much more needs to be done to better support children in this area.

Children and young people are still developing their identity, values and capacity for self-regulation; they are therefore more open to risk taking (Nyström and Bengtsson, 2016). This, combined with dissociative anonymity and the online disinhibition effect (Suler, 2004), can augment young people's readiness to adopt risky behaviour (Megele with Buzzi, 2017a) or to share personal details and private information online. Indeed, one of the most common risks for children and young people is 'friending' or communicating with people they don't know online (Livingstone, 2008).

There are also questions about the effects of digital media and social networking sites (SNS) on young people's growth and psychosocial wellbeing. A study of 750 students in grades 7 to 12 revealed that heavy social media use was associated with mental health difficulties among participants (Sampasa-Kanyinga and Lewis, 2015). However, SNS which may seem a source of problem can also be part of the solution. Indeed, given young people's online presence, SNS can offer a place for public health and other services to reach out, connect, communicate and engage them and to offer heath support and promote healthy routines among them.

Peer socialisation is an important feature of adolescence and plays a central role in development of young people's identity. Digital and social media technologies offer unlimited possibilities for such socialisations. Indeed, in developing their sense of self, children and young people experiment with different identities and relationships, and digital and social media technologies offer great flexibility and fluidity in creating and experimenting with different identities and online personas and relationships (Marwick and boyd, 2011). It is understandable that online identities, participations, communications, and socialisations have become such a central concern for children and young people. Furthermore, children's online engagement is integral to their digital rights and indispensable for developing their new media literacies and their digital citizenship. Conversely, digital exclusion and digital inequalities are a new form of prejudice and the source of new vulnerabilities that can have a far-reaching and longitudinal impact in children's lives.

Therefore, it is essential that assessments include appropriate consideration of young people's digital access and digital enablement (Children's Commissioner, 2017; Megele with Buzzi, 2017a). For example, Helsper and Reisdorf (2017) analyses of Swedish and British data note that motivations for being offline changed between 2005 and 2013 among social media non-users and ex-users and that non-user populations have become more concentrated in vulnerable groups.

However, digital and social media engagement also exposes children to numerous risks, ranging from sexting and sexual solicitation to cyberbullying and online aggression, violence and abuse. Hence, effective safeguarding of children while supporting their healthy growth and development both online and offline is an integral part of social work practice. The 10 Cs model of risk and resilience typology offers a systematic classification of online risks that enable practitioners to adopt a holistic and evidence-informed approach to assessments and protection of children and young people; the 10 Cs risk and resilience typology was developed as a result of a multi-year research project involving hundreds of practitioners and children and young people, examining numerous case studies and is being used by practitioners in local authorities and schools for a systemic and person-centred classification of online risks (see Megele with Buzzi, 2017a).

The medium of play and its importance for children and young people

Children and young people learn about themselves and their world through the medium of play (Winnicott, 1975[1953]:2); digital and social media technologies offer great, and virtually unlimited, possibilities for play online. In this sense, digital and social media can be thought of as a vast and diverse playground where the possibilities for play are limited only by one's imagination. This clearly represents enormous potential for learning, self-development and growth and, therefore, is exciting, intriguing, fascinating and deeply engaging for children and young people.

However, whereas the perimeter of physical playgrounds and playrooms are well defined, it is difficult to establish clear boundaries for children's online engagement. This difficulty in demarcating a 'safe zone' for children's online activities and interactions leaves them vulnerable to a host of undesirable factors, including exposure to indecent, inappropriate or harmful content, sexual solicitations and sexting, or cyberbullying or other forms of aggression and abuse. This absence of clear demarcation and boundaries and its associated risks is further complicated by lack of adult supervision. Indeed, as discussed in Megele with Buzzi (2017a), individual vulnerabilities combined with access/proximity or contact with a motivated perpetrator or source of harm and inadequate protection and supervision form the 'triangle of harm' that leads to negative outcomes, office online aggression and abuse (Cohen and Felson, 1979). Hence, in most safeguarding cases practitioners can target their interventions in order to prevent the occurrence of harm by preventing the convergence of these three required key elements for occurrence of harm. It is essential that social workers are aware and able use this approach to provide effective intervention, guidance and support to safeguard children and young people both online and offline.

At the time of writing, the authors' experiences indicate that restricting internet access is not an uncommon practice in children's homes and that some parents and practitioners consider social media an unnecessary complicating factor in children's lives and practice more restrictive approaches to use of digital and social media technologies (Buzzi, 2020; Buzzi and Megele, 2020). However, digital access and digital and new media literacies are increasingly a new source of inequality, with great implications for young people's learning and future opportunities. Therefore, assessments and interventions should ensure that children have appropriate digital access and are enabled and adequately supported to develop their new media literacies and enhance their digital citizenship (Sun and Shang, 2014; Verhaeghe et al, 2015; Megele with Buzzi, 2017a).

Furthermore, it is important that employers have a clear digital and social media policy and effective training and support to enable social workers to carry out an assessment of online and offline risks and to promote children's and young people's digital rights and support the development of their digital and new media skills and digital citizenship. As suggested by *Working Together to Safeguard Children* (HM Government, 2018: 12–13): 'To be effective, practitioners need to continue to develop their knowledge and skills in this area and be aware of the new and emerging threats, including online abuse, grooming, sexual exploitation and radicalisation.' However, the absence of a systematic approach and understanding of online risk and lack of a clear methodology for assessing online risks has been a major challenge for parents and professionals alike. Indeed, given social work's mandate of safeguarding and support, social workers should be aware and able to provide informed guidance and support for young people's digital and social media engagements and the 10 Cs model offers an evidence-informed approach for doing so. Furthermore, children's digital development is intertwined with their physical and psychological wellbeing: lack of due and thoughtful consideration of online risks and of children's and young people's online engagements may result in significant harm and may be construed as a lack of due diligence.

Example: the case of Tallulah Wilson

Tallulah Mary Scarlett WILSON was 15 years old when she jumped in front of a train and killed herself. The Regulation 28: Prevention of Future Deaths report (2014) sent to Jeremy Hunt, Secretary of Health at the time indicates:

> The jury found that, as a result of Tallulah's dissatisfaction with her friendship group, she created an online persona.
>
> She posted about self harm and suicide. She included photographs that she said were of herself following cutting.
>
> Her consultant psychiatrist gave evidence that, with hindsight, it seems that when her Tumblr account was deleted (following her mother's discovery of the damaging nature of her posts), Tallulah

may have felt herself to be in some way deleted. Thousands of people had read her posts and she had gained great satisfaction from that. So on the one hand, her internet use may have had a negative impact; and yet on the other hand, preventing her internet use may have had a negative impact.

The jury included the following in the narrative determination. 'This case has highlighted the importance of online life for young people. We all have a responsibility to gain a better understanding of this, which needs to be achieved through appropriate dialogue. This is a particular challenge for health professionals and educators.'

CORONER'S CONCERNS

During the course of the inquest, the evidence revealed matters giving rise to concern. In my opinion, there is a risk that future deaths will occur unless action is taken. In the circumstances, it is my statutory duty to report to you.

The **MATTERS OF CONCERN** are as follows.

Although Tallulah was treated by a number of healthcare professionals, and her mother was extremely concerned about her wellbeing, no person who gave evidence felt that, at the time they were looking after Tallulah, they had a good enough understanding of the evolving way that the internet is used by young people, most particularly in terms of the online life that is quite separate from, but sometimes seems to be used to try to validate, the rest of life.'

Unfortunately, the tragic story of Tallulah is not an isolated case and demonstrates that lack of due attention and understanding of practice implications of technology result in inadequate safeguarding and can lead to tragic outcomes.

Social media's importance for young people's development, relationships and identity

Sense of belongingness and self-disclosure are two important identity-supporting processes that are central to young people's identity development. These processes are particularly important in adolescence, when questions of identity and a search for 'who one is' and 'how one fits into one's social and environmental context and the world' become the main focus of the individual (Buzzi and Megele, 2011). The answers to these questions form the foundation of individuals' adult identity and experiences and are linked to their psychological wellbeing. Indeed, in his psychosocial studies, Erikson (1968, 1980) asserts that the primary task of adolescence is the formation of a personally meaningful and socially validated identity.

Through peer interactions, adolescents establish and reinforce shared norms and define themselves in relation to their peers and as distinct from their parents. Through shared symbolisms (such as clothing and music), norms and behaviours, adolescents develop and sustain a sense of belonging with their peers who share their interests and values (Brechwald and Prinstein, 2011) and the 24-hour connectivity of digital and social media support adolescents' experiences of peer relationships.

Mobile phones, SNS, texting and other instant messaging systems provide a continuous connection and create a sense of co-presence between friends and peers, while SNS such as Facebook, Instagram, Flickr, Pinterest and so on enable young people to 'hang out' together in a more public way; for example, by livestreaming their daily lives and experiences, posting images of themselves with their friends, leaving messages on each other's social media pages, listing their friends on their profiles, and liking each other's posts and pages (boyd, 2007; Livingstone and Haddon, 2009; Weinstein, 2018).

Sustaining and strengthening a young person's sense of belonging are central to their wellbeing and healthy development; research suggests that adolescents' online communication and interactions with peers has a positive effect on their quality of life (Hsu et al, 2018).

Self-disclosure is another developmentally important task that is the focus of adolescence. Many young people use digital and social media to engage in self-disclosure with their close friends, and longitudinal studies suggest that instant messaging increases the tendency for intimate self-disclosure (Valkenburg and Peter, 2009). Textual and symbolic interactions (such as pictures and likes) and asynchronous communication reduce the cognitive load/demand that is associated with face-to-face interactions and generate a feeling of ease which facilitates self-disclosure (Megele, 2014; Walther, 2007); anonymity can also facilitate self-disclosure. While these processes are supportive of children and young people's development, research also indicates that over-exposure to SNS may trigger feelings of envy and promote narcissistic behaviour which, in turn, can negatively affect their wellbeing and life satisfaction (Krasnova et al, 2013).

The above underline the importance of social media for children's and young people's identity and as developmental processes. This also highlights the need for social workers and safeguarding professionals and practitioners working with children and young people to be digitally enabled and to have a good appreciation and understanding of these processes and other relevant challenges and opportunities offered by digital and social media technologies.

Dark play

In spite of their many benefits, digital and social media technologies and SNS are also used for transgression of boundaries, crime, aggression, and abuse such as cyberbullying, online grooming, and 'dark play'. Dark play refers to the creation of 'fictional' or 'pseudo' characters online with the intention to deceive others (Megele with Buzzi, 2017a). The following example offers a glimpse into dark play, and is also an example of when the rights and boundaries of children and young people and their families are violated in a mindless manner.

#BabyRP

Games such as #BabyRP are an example of some of challenges associated with social media posting. #BabyRP is a game in which photos of babies are harvested/copied from other people's social media accounts and reposted under a different account with a new name and imaginary storyline, inviting others to role-play being daddy, mummy or child.

Players argue that they get the pictures from social media accounts that are public and that this means that the pictures are public too and, therefore, that they are allowed to use them. Players offer a variety of motivations for engaging in such role plays, ranging from wanting to be someone else who is loved to missing being a child, to just having a good time. But, most players seem to be adolescents and young people role-playing to be parents. But it is not difficult to find sexualised versions of #BabyRP. Clearly, this is distressing for parents who are unaware that the photo of their child is being used in that manner and usually only find out when it is too late.

Possible precautions for parents and practitioners to avoid/prevent being victimised by #BabyRP or similar sort of games are to follow good practice advice that applies to most online/virtual activities. In general, it is good practice to:

- be mindful and think carefully about what one is posting and who it is shared with;
- be sure to keep accounts private and do not accept friends or followers that one does not know;
- watermark all images/photos, especially if they are being shared more widely;
- ensure that location tagging is turned off.

Sexting

The concept of sexting is no longer limited to the use of mobile phones. Instead it is more broadly defined as 'sexually explicit content communicated via text messages, smartphones, or visual and web 2.0 activities such as social networking sites' (Ringrose et al, 2012, p 9).

The main risk with sexting is that images and sexts could be forwarded to an audience wider than the one intended by the producer of the sext. This can damage the person's reputation and image and can lead to undesired sexual solicitation, cyberbullying or other abuse.

Although the exchange of self-produced sexually explicit images within the context of relationships or harassment cases is not a new phenomenon (Chalfen, 2009), digital and social media technologies have dramatically transformed its potential for replication and further distribution as well as its consequences for the person's image and identity. For instance, the recipient of a sext can forward the message to others or can post it on social media, blogs, photo sharing platforms, or even pornography websites.

Such actions could be driven by a host of motives including demonstrating one's popularity and gaining peer approval, or as part of a game and 'just for fun', to expressing intimacy or revenge for a relationship that has gone sour. However, regardless of motives, such actions can have far reaching consequences. Indeed, once an image or a message is posted online, it is almost impossible to retrieve or to know how many people have seen or copied and/or redistributed that message. This poses a huge challenge for safeguarding practitioners in relation to online posts and sexting message. For example, in 2016/17 alone there were 21,511 visits to the information and advice pages on the Childline website about online grooming.

Studies indicate (Dake et al, 2012; Rice et al, 2012) that sexting is correlated with a number of other risk-taking behaviours, for example:

- young people who engaged in sexting had a greater likelihood of sexual activity and of having unprotected sex;
- young people who engaged in sexting had an increased risk of becoming the target of cyberbullying;
- sexting has also been associated with the use of alcohol, marijuana, and smoking cigarettes.

Another study involving 12- to 18-year-olds suggests that sexting may lead to sadness and hopelessness as well as suicide and suicidal ideations. However, it is not clear as to whether sexting precedes or follows such risks, and further research is needed in this area.

Notwithstanding, there are different interpretations of and reasons for engaging in sexting; Lenhart found that some young people argue that sexting is 'a safer alternative to real life sexual activity' (2009, p 8) while others argue that sexting is a way of documenting one's sexuality (Hasinoff, 2012); some researchers argue that, from a socio-cultural perspective, sexting could be considered as a by-product of technological convergence and a form of remediation of body and identity in a way that generates specific forms of user-generated capital (Curnutt, 2012). In a world of text-based communication, sexting is a form of sexual expression documenting the sexuality of the individual in contemporary digital culture. (See Megele with Buzzi [2017a] for a more detailed discussion of sexting.)

Practice implications of sexting

Given the dissemination potential of digital and social media technologies and its associated risks, sexting may have significant, lasting and far-reaching implications with multiple negative outcomes for its subjects (Ringrose et al, 2012). In such circumstances, practitioners need to ensure multi-professional working involving the parents or carers, the police, the school and any other person as need be to ensure children and young people are adequately supported and effectively safeguarded. It is also important to know when to seek legal advice regarding such cases.

The school plays an important role in prevention as well as intervention and support plan in response to sexting cases. Therefore, schools should have clear anti-sexting policies and prevention strategies and, in their sex education or digital citizenship classes, should inform and educate young people about the negative consequences of sexting. This information can be included in the school's PSHE education and in line with the statutory guidance by the Department of Education (DfE, 2019). Given the complexities and sensitivities involved in sexting behaviour and its implications and the gendered motivations for and consequences of sexting (Ringrose et al, 2012), it is also important that schools offer separate (same-sex and/or gendered-focus) classes when discussing sexting.

It is important to engage with and investigate the person misusing/abusing texting as this may reveal other victims who may need intervention and support. Practitioners should act with discretion and sensitivity, and avoid judgemental attitudes and criminalising young people who may be involved in sexting; such young people will need re-education and rehabilitation in relation to their sexting behaviour. Practitioners should also be mindful to avoid a 'blame the victim' attitude where the producers of sexts (these are mostly girls) (Ringrose et al, 2012) are blamed or shamed for the consequences of sexting.

There are a number of video testimonials on YouTube by victims of sexting speaking about their ordeal and how they coped with it. These testimonials can offer a point of departure for discussing the impact of sexting and the spread of messages (Lippman and Campbell, 2014). The Share Aware campaign run by the NSPCC offers a range of information and resources to help parents speak with their children about staying safe on SNS (for details see NSPCC, 2015).

As suggested in Megele with Buzzi (2017a), some of the starting points in working with sexting situations involve identifying: who and how many were involved in sexting; the type and nature of sexting (for example, text, picture, partial or fully nude images, images of sexual intercourse, screen shots of images, and so on); how the sexting began and why was it sent; what was the context of sexting (for example, game, flirting, intimate relationship, bullying, voyeurism, and so on); what was the platform for communication and dissemination – that is, how was the original message sent and how was it subsequently distributed (for example, shown visually but not disseminated, forwarded to others, posted on a website or SNS, and so on). Sexting victims should be provided with appropriate support and this could be complemented with a list of contacts and helpful resources, including self-help resources, that they may draw upon to stay safe. The NSPCC and Barnardo's offer a range of resources, information and support including online advice, advocacy, helpline and online counselling that can be helpful for both parents and children (see services and resources on NSPCC.org.uk and Barnardos.org.uk).

As is the case with cyberbullying, it is important to note, and to inform sexting victims, that retaliation against a perpetrator is not an effective strategy. Instead, if the person abusing sexting is a young person, practitioners should contact him/her and his/her parents to ensure parents are informed and that appropriate support and rehabilitative measures have been put in place; practitioners can use the 10 Cs risk and resilience toolkit as an interactive tool in working with, supporting and safeguarding children and young people (see esafeguarding.org for the relevant tools).

Many young people think that sexting is the norm amongst their peers (Lippman and Campbell, 2014). Therefore, it is essential to highlight to them that this is not the case and that the majority of young people do not engage in sexting (Ringrose et al, 2012). Practitioners should also consider that at times young people receive a sext message without having sought or solicited it and may experience peer pressure to forward/disseminate the message.

There is a resurgence of patriarchal values and division of gender roles in sexting behaviour. Therefore, practitioners should be aware of the gendered implications of sexting (that is, often the attitude toward sexting and its consequences are different for boys than for girls): young men may collect sext messages or even post their own sexually explicit images as a sign of their popularity and masculinity with this leading to their increased social capital and popularity among their peers; young women are usually the main producer of sexting messages and are often the subject of sexting and posting of their sexually explicit images is usually viewed negatively by their peers and leads to their unpopularity with other young women (Ringrose et al, 2012; see Megele with Buzzi, 2017a for case examples and further discussion of sexting).

Similar to bullying, peer group reactions have significant implications for sexting behaviour and its impact among young people. Therefore, educating young people to challenge and report peers who spread sexting messages can serve as an important protective factor. Young people should feel enabled and supported to express open disapproval of sexting messages and to refuse to forward such messages. They should also feel empowered to seek help about and report such behaviour; parents and professionals play a crucial role in this regard.

This underlines the importance of appropriate training for practitioners and for them to have a clear strategy as well as specific and flexible guideline and emergency plans for responding to sexting or other forms of abuse or aggression or other negative online or offline behaviours. Practitioners need to be able to recognise the sensitivities, impact and implications, and legal liabilities for those involved in sexting behaviour. Sexting victims may need counselling and support for coping with the situation as well as practical support and advice from practitioners or other professionals with regards to the appropriate course of action including privacy and identity management (see esafeguarding.org for the 10 Cs risk and resilience toolkit and examples of practical support for sexting); it is important to work sensitively and collaboratively with sexting victims to stop and remediate the situation and mitigate its consequences and to gather evidence.

Cyberbullying

Peer group play a fundamental role in young people's socialisation and social identity development and serve as a source of validation and social reference. The role of peers is particularly significant during adolescence when peer socialisation is central to the processes of growth and identity formation (Hatano et al, 2016). Through the use of social media and online interactions, adolescents generate a feeling of togetherness and a sense of social acceptance, popularity and being surrounded by friends; this helps regulate emotions and generate positive self-evaluation and regard, as well as serving as a mechanism to contain an individual's anxieties and depressions (Buzzi and Megele, 2020). Indeed, through use of digital and social media, adolescents acquire emotional support and develop intimate relationships and a sense of belonging and peer acceptance. Such attachments and social bonds are associated with prosocial behaviours (Barry and Wentzel, 2006). Given the importance of peer acceptance and validation during adolescence, cyberbullying can be particularly devastating at this time: it not only represents a rejection and othering of the individual, it is also – given the ubiquity of social media – all-invasive and is often experienced as incessant, omnipresent and influencing the young person's experiences continuously and at all times. The young person's online presence and identity are violated without boundary, be it on the street or in the privacy of one's home, and this leaves no safe haven for the individual.

Cyberbullying represents a significant and complex challenge for children, parents and practitioners; as far back as 2014, almost 45,000 children and young people talked to ChildLine about bullying, while in 2016/17 Childline conducted 2,422 counselling sessions with young people due to bullying on SNS and games platforms (private communication, 2017); many experts believe that the majority of children and young people will experience cyber-aggression and bullying at some point.

Risk factors for cyberbullying

In assessing the risk factors and when planning for safeguarding children and young people from cyberbullying, it is important to distinguish between static and dynamic risk factors.

By definition, **static risk factors** are those that cannot change and remain the same – they are usually rooted in an individual's history (for example, family, care experience) or unchanging demographic features. Gender is a static factor and data suggest that boys are more involved as cyberbullies than girls. Other static risk factors include: prior experience of bullying or other antisocial behaviour, prior victimisation, past exposure to violence, and impulsivity.

Dynamic risk factors can change either with time or through specific measures and/or interventions (Andrews and Bonta, 2006). Parental supervision and academic performance and achievement represent dynamic risk factors. Others include:

- School policies and commitment and environmental factors, such as the attitudes, routines and behaviour of adults in the school environment. These play a major role in determining the extent to which the problems will manifest themselves in a classroom or a school (Olweus and Limber, 2010).
- The extent of technology use is highly associated with cyberbullying. Studies (Livingstone et al, 2011) indicate that the more time spent online, the more the probability of experience of cyberbullying. This is clearly a dynamic risk factor that can be rectified with better management regulating the amount of time, frequency and quality of the person's digital and social media engagement.
- Risky online behaviour is a dynamic risk factor. Research indicates a significant correlation between young people

engaging in risky behaviour – such as surfing and using unsuitable or age-inappropriate contents or websites, or connecting with and friending strangers on SNS – and being a cyberbully (Van Ouytsel et al, 2017).

- Personality is a dynamic risk factor and lower levels of empathy, low self-esteem, and low self-regulation and control are associated with higher rates of cyberbullying.
- Individual and family values is a dynamic risk factor. Specifically, moral disengagement as manifested in denial of wrongdoing, moral detachment about antisocial behaviour or attitudes toward blaming the victim, and so on, are associated with cyberbullying. Cyberbullies tend to break rules more often than non-cyberbullies. Cyberbullies often distort values, resulting in normative beliefs that justify or condone aggression or minimise its effect (Kowalski et al, 2014). Other indications include maladaptive or externalising behaviour (for example, use of alcohol or antisocial behaviour).

Finding and communicating with birth parents

A study by NAO (2014) states that as many as two thirds of children who are in foster or adopted families have been removed from their birth families due to significant neglect or abuse and a situation that could not have been remedied through additional support and services. In many such 'closed' adoptions, communication between adopted children and their birth parents usually goes through a 'letterbox process' mediated by social workers. In other words, the adoptive parents send the birth family a letter and some photos every year through a social worker or adoption agency as intermediary and any response from the birth parents goes through the same route. However, social media and SNS such as Facebook and Twitter have changed this landscape dramatically. Both adopted children and their birth families can now search for each other through SNS and using photos or other information such as name, date of birth or location information.

In a report by the Channel 4 News, one adoptive mother highlighted how a message to her daughter from the birth mother had had a catastrophic impact on her family. The adoptive mother explained:

> 'Our daughter, who is our prime concern, has gone from no contact from her birth family, at the hands of whom she had a difficult start in life, to suddenly finding they are there at the press of a button.'

The young person had just turned 16 when she received a message via SNS, shortly before she was due to sit her GCSEs. This text message caused a great deal of emotional distress; the adoptive mum indicated that it had "completely thrown her". The birth mother painted a skewed picture of the adoption circumstances without acknowledging the years of abuse and neglect that had led to her daughter being removed from the family at the age of seven. This contact by the birth mother resulted in substantial difficulties for the daughter.

Such situations are further complicated by the way 'life story books' try to depict a more positive picture of the birth parents than the actual experiences of the children who have been removed from their families. However, this diluted version of what happened to them generates at least two important problems. First, on a psychological level, it results in 'splitting' (black and white thinking) as the children are unable to reconcile the more positive depiction of their birth families as reflected in their life story book with their conscious and unconscious experiences of the severe and significant trauma, neglect and abuse that experienced while with their birth parents. Second, for some children who may have repressed or suppressed their memories of neglect and abuse, or were too young to remember, or prefer to believe the story book version of 'reality', this may lead to a desire to re-establish contact with their birth parent prematurely, before they are emotionally and psychologically ready to do so. This can generate a host of problems, ranging from disappointment to deep feelings of rejection and emotional difficulties that can lead to the breakdown of adoptions. The same risks may apply to fostering arrangements.

Many adoption and fostering agencies and services have recognised the need to tell the truth to children and young people in an age-appropriate manner so they are aware of the actual reasons, causes and circumstances that led to their removal from their birth families and subsequent placement with foster parents and/or adoption. In this process, children and their adoptive families need to be supported by appropriate services and practitioners with expertise in childhood trauma to ensure children and young people are able to make sense of the neglect and abuse that they experienced and to enhance their protection and resilience in relation to inappropriate or intrusive contacts.

Another problem is that, at times, birth parents or others share photos of children with a narrative that may not correspond to the child's story with an appeal for help to find their 'long lost child'. This depiction is clearly far removed from the harsh realities that many adopted children had to face before their removal and placement in a new foster or adopted family that could love them, care for them and meet their needs. However, other people on SNS, without knowing the context and background of the child, out of good will and in sympathy with parents may share such information leading to thousands of likes and shared posts, and giving substantial visibility to the parents' appeal and facilitating their discovery by children and young people.

Unfortunately, often these contacts are far from what the child may have imagined and may lead to complex feelings and emotional difficulties that can have a significant impact on their traumatised and recovering identities. If the young person and their foster carer or adoptive families are not adequately supported and their difficulties effectively addressed, this can lead to challenging and externalising behaviour and can strain the positive relationship and the attachment bonds between such children and their foster/adoptive parents. Unfortunately in some cases this can lead to the breakdown of the adoption and/or foster placement.

The government response has recognised the new challenges posed by social media and SNS, and the legislation enables adopters to apply for a no-contact order if they feel inappropriate contact is taking place. This legislation is designed with social media in mind and with the intention of protecting children and young people. However, more needs to be done and indeed,

'... the erosion in the hitherto impermeable seal around the adoptive placement created by social media' requires a new approach and mindset (McFarlane, 2017, p 17). This remains one of the most important challenges for adoption and fostering in the 21st century.

Online grooming

In addition to its many positive potentials, digital and social media technologies can also entail negative outcomes and offer opportunities for grooming, aggression or criminal exploitation (Taylor and Quayle, 2006), and for children and young people to take sexual risks. This is further complicated by the effect of technology, as research indicates that use of technology affects the individual's mood, thinking and behaviour (Buzzi and Megele, 2020). For instance, there is increasing concern that use of SNS may be associated with increased exposure and risk of harm for children and young people. Many sexual offenders routinely use technology to complete everyday tasks and as part of their everyday lives and therefore have the technical knowhow and are able to create private cyberspaces for themselves, their fantasies and behaviours. An NSPCC study (Bentley et al, 2017, p 29), comparing the data between 2015/16 and 2014/15, indicates that:

- There is a 30% increase in rape of a male under 13 (from 1,268 to 1,648).
- Sexual activity involving a child under 16 has increased by 32% (from 8,051 to 10,661).

Although the above figures are not limited to online grooming, they provide an indication of a problematic trend. Indeed, in 2016/17 there were 12,248 Childline counselling sessions about online safety and abuse, representing a 9% increase on the previous year (private communication, 2017).

Interviews with offenders reveal that they use children's and young people's online profiles to search for targets with particular physical, psychological and behavioural characteristics. Offenders use digital and social media technologies and SNS to initiate contact, establish relationships, communicate, and access information as well as to disseminate information about their target and contact the target's friends. Perpetrators often hid behind the guise of anonymity and the possibility of holding multiple online identities. More importantly, the omnipresence of digital and social media technology offers new possibilities for social interactions in new and diverse contexts, while transforming the nature and notion of such interactions. Such social affordances, including 'sexual behaviour, [as well as other types of behaviour] ... depend on the perceiving of what another person or other persons afford, or sometimes on the misperceiving of it' (Gibson, 1979, p 135). However, the affordances of technology are not neutral and do not exist in vacuum. Instead it is important to consider their possible implications and when and by whom and for whom they might be used.

Research indicates that offenders use different approaches and strategies and although an offender may start with chatrooms and may engage in multiple conversations, they will usually aim to create a private space between themselves and the young person. For example, they may invite the young person to move to MSN or to use the webcam. This transition allows for synchronicity and a sense of privacy and/or intimacy that offers fertile ground for further exploitation. The combination of textual and mobile (for example, pay as you go) communication offers a further layer of protection for offenders, enabling them to hide their identities and trail and manipulate technology to avoid detection.

Many offenders play out their fantasies online, while others progress to face-to-face meetings with their target. However, the offenders' deceptions often span name, age, physical appearance, and interests, with many offenders using multiple identities and presenting themselves with different personas based on the target's online profile and interest. The age deception is at times required in order to gain access to younger people's chatrooms and other cyberspaces; if the deception is ever uncovered, then the offender will simply abandon that identity and create/ use a different profile. However, there are many variations in approach, and even cases where offenders have revealed their real identity to their target.

In response to these threats, there are a number of important initiatives and resources to safeguard children and young people. For example, in August 2015, the Internet Watch Foundation (*Wired*, 10 August 2015) announced that it could provide 'hashes' (a tag or function that helps map data) of child sexual abuse images to Google, Twitter and Facebook to speed up the identification and removal of images online, including preventing images from being uploaded in the first place or being repeatedly shared. Furthermore, artificial intelligence is being used with increasing accuracy to identify child sexual abuse images online. These and other technologies are used by the UK's National Crime Agency Command, Child Exploitation and Online Protection Command (CEOP), to protect children and young people both online and offline.

Another example, is NSPCC Net Aware (Net-Aware.org.uk) which is addressed to parents of 8- to 12-year-olds and offers a guide for SNS, apps or games that children use most frequently. This guide was developed in collaboration between NSPCC and Mumsnet and is the result of consultation with 2,361 children and young people about their most popular SNS and apps and what they thought of them. It also involved over 500 parents who reviewed these SNS and shared their views, rating each site for its safety advice, signing up, reporting and privacy settings.

Conclusion

Social work and social care may have been slow in adopting digital and social media technologies; however, digital and social media technologies are an integral part of children's and young people's lives and identities and play an increasingly important role in safeguarding cases. Therefore, it is essential that social workers and social care professionals recognise the importance and the powerful, transformational and developmental implications, challenges and opportunities associated with digital and social media technologies. Knowledge and Skills Statement (KSS) 5 for newly qualified social workers recognises the need for holistic safeguarding of children. Indeed, failure to consider holistic safeguarding of children and young people, both online and offline, may lead to significant harm and may be construed as professional neglect or lack of due diligence.

The United Nations Convention on the Rights of the Child (UNCRC) is an international human rights treaty to which the UK is a signatory, which grants all children and young people below the age of 18 a comprehensive set of rights including the right to 'develop their personality, abilities and talents to the fullest potential'. Consequently, the Children Act 1989 requires that local authorities should enable and support children and young people within their authority so they are able to achieve their full potential. If we do not enable and equip children with the digital capabilities, knowledge, skills and experiences that are indispensable for their healthy and holistic growth and digital citizenship while protecting them from risks of adverse outcomes both online and offline, then we are depriving them of better future opportunities and impacting their life chances negatively – and in effect failing to safeguard children and young people adequately.

Given the widespread use of digital and social media technologies by children and young people, it is urgent that we make this a priority in the national curriculum and in line with the statutory guidance from DfE (2019). It is equally urgent that e-safety and digital and online safeguarding are embedded in social work curricula and for social workers and other professionals working with children and young people to enhance their digital and social media literacy and have a good understanding of the advantages as well as challenges posed by digital and social media technologies, so they can provide the necessary knowledge, engagement, support, and guidance for children and young people and use technology in a professional and contextually relevant manner.

Social workers need to take the time to understand the impact of social media on children's and young people's lives and in the way they relate to technology and use it seamlessly for living, learning and socialising. Alternatively, there is the risk of isolating and alienating practitioners from children's and young people's lives and experiences and jeopardising their own ability to adequately safeguard children. Such a gap in social workers' knowledge and capabilities can lead to reduced influence and de-professionalisation of social work. As suggested by Masson et al (2013, pp 24–40) there is the danger of the profession trapping itself 'in a twentieth-century mind-set (relying on postal addresses and landline numbers) when their clients are using twenty-first-century means of communication'.

It is both urgent and of fundamental importance that social workers enhance their digital citizenship and develop their digital professionalism so that they are technically enabled, ethically informed and professionally prepared to respond, support, safeguard and manage young people's needs and wellbeing and to respond adequately to the challenges and opportunities of digital and social media technologies and to safeguard and support children and young people both online and offline in an effective, timely and purposeful manner.

Finally, it is essential that social media companies should take a more proactive and responsive role in challenging and removing hateful, aggressive or abusive content. Given the inadequacy of self-regulation on the part of social media companies. Ofcom's new and added responsibility for regulation of online social media platforms is an important step in the right direction and can be further strengthened by the Children's Commissioner's proposal for the establishment of a 'digital ombudsman' to mediate between children and social media companies over the removal of content. Such an ombudsman can provide a much needed, and currently lacking, online support for children and young people and their families (see Children's Commissioner, 2017).

References

Andrews D. A. and Bonta J. (2006) *The Psychology of Criminal Conduct* (4th edn). Newark, NJ: LexisNexis.

Barnardos (2019) *Left to their own Devices: Children's social media and mental health.* Available at: https://www.barnardos.org.uk/campaign-with-us/childrens-social-media-and-mental-health

Barry, C. and Wentzel, K. (2006) 'Friend influence on prosocial behavior: The role of motivational factors and friendship characteristics', *Development Psycholology*, 42(1): 153–63.

Bentley, H., Burrows, A., Hafizi, M., Kumari, P., Mussen, N., O'Hagan, O. and Peppiate, J. (2017) *How Safe Are Our Children? The most comprehensive overview of child protection in the UK 2017*. London: NSPCC. Available at: https://www.nspcc.org.uk/globalassets/documents/research-reports/how-safe-children-2017-report.pdf

boyd, danah (2007) 'Why youth (heart) social network sites: The role of networked publics in teenage social life', in D. Buckingham (ed) *MacArthur Foundation Series on Digital Learning – Youth, Identity, and Digital Media Volume*. Cambridge, MA: MIT Press.

Brechwald, W. and Prinstein, M. (2011) 'Beyond homophily: A decade of advances in understanding peer influence processes', *Journal of Research on Adolescence*, 21(1): 166–79.

Buzzi, P. (2020) *Relationship based Practice in Digital Age*. London: PSW Network.

Buzzi, P. and Megele, C. (2011) 'Reflections on the 21st century migrant: Impact of social networking and hyper-reality on the lived experience of global migration' in M. German and P. Banerjee (eds) *Migration, Technology and Transculturation: A Global Perspective*. St. Charles, MO: Lindenwood University Press.

Buzzi, P. and Megele, C. (2020) *Digital Practice and Working with Children and Young People Online*. London: PSW Network.

Chalfen, R. (2009) '"It's only a picture": Sexting, "smutty" snapshots and felony charges', *Visual Studies*, 24(3): 258–68.

Children's Commissioner (2017) 'Foreword' in C. Megele with P. Buzzi, *Safeguarding Children and Young People Online*. Bristol: Policy Press.

Cohen, L., and Felson, M. (1979) 'Social change and crime rate trends: a routine activity approach', *American Sociological Review*, 44(4).

Curnutt, H. (2012) 'Flashing your phone: Sexting and the remediation of teen sexuality', *Communication Quarterly*, 60(3): 353–69.

Dake, J., Price, J., Maziarz, L. and Ward. B. (2012) 'Prevalence and correlates of sexting behavior in adolescents', *American Journal of Sexuality Education*, 7(1): 1–15.

DfE (2019) *Keeping Children Safe in Education: Statutory guidance for schools and colleges*. Available at: https://assets.publishing.service.gov.uk/government/uploads/system/uploads/attachment_data/file/835733/Keeping_children_safe_in_education_2019.pdf

Erikson, E. H. (1968) *Identity, Youth, and Crisis*. New York: Norton.

Erikson, E. H. (1980) *Identity and the Life Cycle* (reissue). New York: Norton.

Gibson, J. (1979) *The Ecological Approach to Visual Perception*. Boston: Houghton Mifflin Company.

Haraway, D. (1991) *Simians, Cyborgs and Women: The Reinvention of Nature* (2nd edn). London: Free Association Books.

Hasinoff, A. (2012) 'Sexting as media production: Rethinking social media and sexuality', *New Media & Society*, 15(4): 449–65.

Hatano, K., Sugimura, K. and Crocetti, E. (2016) 'Looking at the dark and bright sides of identity formation: New insights from adolescents and emerging adults in Japan', *Journal of Adolescence*, 47: 156–68.

Helsper, E. and Reisdorf, B. (2017) 'The emergence of a "digital underclass" in Great Britain and Sweden: Changing reasons for digital exclusion', *New Media & Society*, 19(8): 1253–70.

HM Government (2018) *Working Together to Safeguard Children: A guide to inter-agency working to safeguard and promote the welfare of children*. Available at: https://assets.publishing.service.gov.uk/government/uploads/system/uploads/attachment_data/file/779401/Working_Together_to_Safeguard-Children.pdf

Hsu, M. S. H., Rouf, A. and Allman-Farinelli, M. (2018) 'Effectiveness and behavioral mechanisms of social media interventions for positive nutrition behaviors in adolescents: A systematic review', *Journal of Adolescent Health*, 63(5): 531–45.

Kowalski, R., Giumetti, G., Schroeder, A. and Lattanner, M. (2014) 'Bullying in the digital age: A critical review and meta-analysis of cyberbullying research among youth', *Psychological Bulletin*, 140(4): 1073–137.

Krasnova, H., Wenninger, H., Widjaja, T. and Buxmann, P. (2013) 'Envy on Facebook: A hidden threat to users' life satisfaction?' *Wirtschaftsinformatik Proceedings 2013*. 92. Available at: http://aisel.aisnet.org/wi2013/92

Lenhart, A. (2009) *Teens and Sexting: How and Why Minor Teens Are Sending Sexually Suggestive Nude or Nearly Nude Images via Text Messaging*. Pew Internet & American Life Project. Available at: https://www.pewinternet.org/2009/12/15/teens-and-sexting/

Lippman, J. R., and Campbell. S. W. (2014) 'Damned if you do, damned if you don't … if you're a girl: Relational and normative contexts of adolescent sexting in the United States', *Journal of Children and Media*, 8(4): 371–86.

Livingstone, S. (2008) 'Taking risky opportunities in youthful content creation: Teenagers' use of social networking sites for intimacy, privacy and self-expression', *New Media & Society*, 10: 393–411.

Livingstone, S. and Haddon, L. (2009) *EU Kids Online: Final report*. LSE, London: EU Kids Online.

Livingstone, S., Haddon, L., Görzig, A. and Ólafsson, K. (2011) *EU Kids*. Available at: www.lse.ac.uk/media%40lse/research/EUKidsOnline/EU%20Kids%20II%20(2009-11)/EUKidsOnlineIIReports/Final%20report.pdf

Marwick, A. and boyd, d. (2011) 'I tweet honestly, I tweet passionately: Twitter users, context collapse, and the imagined audience', *New Media and Society*, 13(1): 114–33.

Masson, H., Balfe, M., Hackett, S. and Phillips, J. (2013) 'Lost without a trace? Social networking and social research with a hard-to-reach population', *British Journal of Social Work*, 43(1): 24–40.

McFarlane, A. (2017) 'Holding the risk: The balance between child protection and the right to family life'. Available at: https://www.judiciary.gov.uk/wp-content/uploads/2017/03/lecture-by-lj-mcfarlane-20160309.pdf

Megele, C. (2014) 'Theorizing Twitter chat', *Journal of Perspectives in Applied Academic Practice*, 2(2). Available at: http://jpaap.napier.ac.uk/index.php/JPAAP/article/view/106/html

Megele. C. with Buzzi, P. (2017a) *Safeguarding Children and Young People Online*. Bristol: Policy Press.

Megele, C. and Buzzi, P. (2017b) *Learning Through Observation: A bio-psychosocial and developmental perspective*. Abingdon: Routledge.

NAO (2014) *Child in Care*. DfE and National Audit Office. Available at: https://www.nao.org.uk/wp-content/uploads/2014/11/Children-in-care1.pdf

NSPCC (2015) 'Share Aware information and resources'. Available at: https://www.nspcc.org.uk/what-we-do/news-opinion/share-aware-campaign-launches/

NSPCC (2016) 'What should I do? NSPCC helplines: responding to children's and parents' concerns about sexual content online'. London: NSPCC. Available at: https://www.nspcc.org.uk/globalassets/documents/research-reports/what-should-i-do-nspcc-helplines-responding-to-childrens-and-parents-concerns-about-sexual-content-online.pdf

Nyström, B. and Bengtsson, H. (2016) 'Temperamental influences on children's risk-taking in decision making: A dual process, multi-level analysis', *Personality and Individual Differences*, (89): 177–81.

Ofcom (2019) *Children's media use and attitudes*. Available at: https://www.ofcom.org.uk/research-and-data/media-literacy-research/childrens

Olweus, D. and Limber, S. (2010) 'Bullying in school: Evaluation and dissemination of the Olweus Bullying Prevention Program', *American Journal of Orthopsychiatry*, 80(1): 124–34.

Rice, E., Rhoades, H., Winetrobe, H., Sanchez, M., Montoya, J., Plant, A. and Kordic, T. (2012) 'Sexually explicit cell phone messaging associated with sexual risk among adolescents', *Pediatrics,* 130(4): 667–73.

Ringrose, J., Gill, R., Livingstone, S. and Harvey, L. (2012) *A Qualitative Study of Children, Young People and 'Sexting': A report prepared for the NSPCC*. UK: National Society for the Prevention of Cruelty to Children.

Sampasa-Kanyinga, H. and Lewis, R. (2015) 'Frequent use of social networking sites is associated with poor psychological functioning among children and adolescents', *Cyberpsychology, Behavior, and Social Networking*, 18(7): 380–5.

Stewart, J. Bleumers, L., Van Looy, J., Mariën, I., All, A., Schurmans, D., Willaert, K., De Grove, F., Jacobs, A., Misuraca, G. and Centeno Mediavilla, I.C. (2013) 'The potential of digital games for empowerment and social inclusion of groups at risk of social and economic exclusion: Evidence and opportunity for policy', *European Commission: Institute for Prospective Technological Studies, JRC Scientific and Policy Reports*. Available at: http://www.most.ie/webreports/2014/oct2014/Potential%20of%20digital%20games%20for%20empowerment%20and%20social%20inclusions%202013.pdf

Suler, J.R. (2004) 'The online disinhibition effect', *Cyberpsychology & Behavior*, 7(3): 321–6.

Sun, Y. and Shang, R. (2014) 'The interplay between users' intraorganizational social media use and social capital', *Computers in Human Behavior*, 37: 334–41.

Taylor, M. and Quayle, E. (2006) 'The Internet and abuse images of children: Search pre-criminal situations and opportunity', in R. Wortley and S. Smallbone (eds), *Situational Prevention of Child Sexual Abuse*. New York, NY: Criminal Justice Press, pp 169–95.

Valkenburg, P. and Peter, J. (2009) 'Social consequences of the internet for adolescents', *Current Directions in Psychological Science*, 18(1): 1–5.

Van Ouytsel, J., Torres, E., Choi, H., Ponnet, K., Walrave, M. and Temple, J. (2017) 'The associations between substance use, sexual behaviors, bullying, deviant behaviors, health, and cyber dating abuse perpetration', *The Journal of School Nursing*, 33(2): 116–22.

Verhaeghe, P., Van der Bracht, K. and Van de Putte, B. (2015) 'Inequalities in social capital and their longitudinal effects on the labour market entry', *Social Networks*, 40: 174–84.

Walther, J. B. (2007) 'Selective self-presentation in computer-mediated communication: Hyperpersonal dimensions of technology, language, and cognition', *Computers in Human Behavior*, 23(5): 2538–57.

Weinstein, E. (2018) 'The social media see-saw: Positive and negative influences on adolescents' affective well-being', *New Media and Society*, 20(10): 3597–623.

Winnicott, D. W. (1975 [1953]) 'Transitional objects and transitional phenomena', in *Through Paediatrics to Psychoanalysis*, London: Karnac Books.

Wired (2015) 'Child sexual abuse "hash lists" shared with internet giants', *Wired* (10 August 2015). Available at: http://www.wired.co.uk/article/iwf-hash-lists-child-abuse-images

4

Social media and adult social work

Peter Buzzi and Sharon Allen

Introduction

One of the primary objectives of adult social work is to support and safeguard adults in order to promote individual autonomy, increase and maximise individual choice, and enhance people's health and wellbeing while ensuring their safety and protection. Adults who access services are often challenged by complex needs and burdened by social stereotypes and stigma that aggravate their difficulties; these include individual vulnerability and human frailty, isolation, social exclusion, social stereotypes and stigma, and so on. These and other challenges may influence people's identity or their ability to meet their own needs, maintain their independence, exercise control, achieve their goals and priorities, and lead healthy and rewarding lives with dignity and integrity. Social media present a host of opportunities to address these and other challenges and to support people in a powerful, transformative and person-centred manner.

This chapter presents a glimpse of some of the applications and transformational implications of digital and social media technologies. It begins by briefly examining adults' use of social media and some of the misconceived assumptions and stereotypes about older adults' use of digital and social media technologies. Challenging Prensky's (2001) notion of digital natives and digital immigrants, it highlights the need for a more critical view and awareness of intersectionality within society (intersectionality refers to interconnected nature of social categorisations such as race, class, gender, ethnicity, religion, age and so on that create overlapping and interdependent experiences and systems of discrimination, oppression, exclusion and disadvantage within society). The chapter then considers the 'social' in health and social care, followed by a discussion of social media and its impact on social capital and relationships. It then offers a brief note about digital storytelling followed by a discussion of social media and people with disabilities with specific focus on social media and autism. This is to demonstrate the transformative power of social media in challenging stigmatising notions of vulnerability and in reframing and repositioning the identity narratives of people who experience difficulties and vulnerabilities or those who may have different modes of information processing. Finally, it presents an example of coproduction and the use of social media to meet an older person's needs, followed by examples of some helpful apps and concludes with a few suggestions for social work and social care practice and education.

Adults' use of social media

A report from Pew Research Center (2017) maintains that, in the US, about 7 in 10 (69%) adult Americans use some type of social media while 67% of adults above 65 years old use the internet. In the UK, 99% of adults between 25–34 have a mobile phone and use the internet and 91% have a social medial profile while among adults between 65–74, 92% have a mobile phone, 67% use the internet and 66% have a social media profile (Ofcom, 2019). However, although 81% of adults aged 75 years old or over have a mobile phone, 48% do not use the internet and only 20% have a social media profile. These statistics suggest that, as of 2019, older adults in the UK are less likely to use the internet than the younger adults.

In general, older people and those in the DE socio-economic group remain less likely to be online and although technology has expanded significantly in recent years, the proportion of adults who do not use the internet is unchanged since 2014 (Ofcom, 2019).

Figure 4.1 highlights the proportion of adults in UK who do not use the internet.

The Ofcom (2019) report does not offer an intersectional analysis of access to and use of the internet and digital and social media technologies. However, considering the many social inequalities in society and the impact of intersectional factors such as race, culture and ethnicity in experience of inequalities, an intersectional analysis of digital access and obstacles to it are rather important. We are further reminded of the significance of such an intersectional analysis if we consider that in a digital society access to digital technology should be a fundamental right for all citizens, and that digital inequalities represent a new source of increasingly important inequality that conditions and limits people's access to valuable information and resources and hampers their ability to meet their needs (Megele and Buzzi, 2017b).

Although there is some indication that age is negatively correlated with internet use among adults in the UK (in other words, older adults are less likely to use the internet than younger

Figure 4.1: UK adults' use of internet

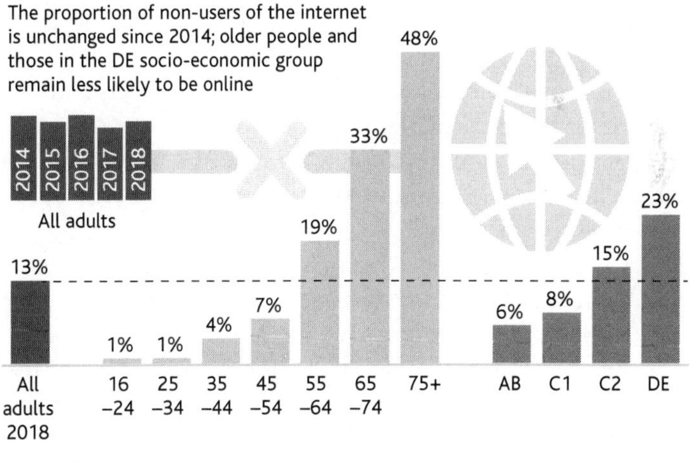

The proportion of non-users of the internet is unchanged since 2014; older people and those in the DE socio-economic group remain less likely to be online

2014 2015 2016 2017 2018

All adults

All adults 2018	16–24	25–34	35–44	45–54	55–64	65–74	75+	AB	C1	C2	DE
13%	1%	1%	4%	7%	19%	33%	48%	6%	8%	15%	23%

Source: Ofcom, 2019, p 19

adults), we suggest that social workers and all relationship-based professions should avoid Prensky's (2001) notions of 'digital natives' and 'digital immigrants'. In his well-known article 'Digital natives, digital immigrants', Prensky suggests that young people today are 'born digital' and are, therefore, different in their thinking about and use of the internet and social media from older generations. However, Prensky's definitions have been challenged and are critiqued as stigmatising (Selwyn, 2009) as he treats young and older adults as monolithic groups (a homogenic group) and constructs a digital divide between young people and older adults when there is no evidence of the homogeneity of 'younger' and 'older' adults (Jones and Shao, 2011). Such an approach to analysis of younger and older adults negates the challenges and differences in access, use and lived experience of adults in relation to the internet and digital technologies. Such stereotypes can also potentially affect the appropriateness of services and skew their effect. If we are to follow the logic of such stereotypes, then as a 'digital immigrant' an adult approaching retirement, who has up-to-date digital skills from their workplace, may be offered the opportunity to access continuous professional development and to participate in basic digital orientation courses which would be useless to them, while a young person who has been looked after and who has not had access to digital technology and does not have the necessary digital knowledge and skills may not receive similar support as they are assumed to be a digital native and therefore adept at use of technology.

Although age is an indicator of likelihood of access and use of digital and social media technologies (Madden and Zickuhr, 2011; Zickuhr and Smith, 2012; Ofcom, 2019; Pew Research Center, 2017), it is important for social work and other relationship-based professions and practitioners to adopt a more critical and holistic perspective in relation to access and use of digital and social media technologies as well as to the many obstacles that may prevent people from using such technologies.

Therefore, it is essential that practitioners avoid stigmatising assumptions and instead maintain an open and enquiring mind and approach to ensure people who access services have digital access and are enabled to use digital and social media technologies in helpful ways to meet their needs and support their autonomy and control as well as health and wellbeing.

Skills for Care's research into digital capabilities (Dunn, 2014) indicates that organisations are at very different stages in how they are embracing social media, with one organisation describing how they use Facebook as a recruitment tool while another organisation encourages workers to actively use Twitter and provides support for them through a Twitter group to ensure that staff have confidence to know what they can and cannot say in the context of their work and roles. Adult social care services' use of Amazon's Echo and Alexa technology (Amazon's artificial intelligence (AI) technology) in order to provide virtual assistance and support for older people is an indication of the many opportunities for enhancement of services afforded by social media technologies (*Portsmouth News*, 2017); such virtual assistance covers a wide variety of possible support, ranging from reminding the person to take their medication to advising them to avoid food that may be harmful for their health to providing companionship or serving as a channel to keep in touch with friends, family or other networks, to enabling e-interventions and more.

The interim findings from the national research and practice development project on digital professionalism and online safeguarding provide an evidence-based view of digital practice in social work and social care. This research (Buzzi, 2020; Buzzi and Megele, 2020) shows that practitioners use a wide variety of social media platforms and Table 4.1 provides a glimpse into some of the social media platforms used by practitioners.

This research demonstrates that practitioners need further training and the opportunity to develop the necessary knowledge and skills to support people who access services in becoming digitally able while safeguarding their wellbeing. Research indicates that there is a divergence of perception and opinion between social workers and their managers in relation to workers' digital skills and confidence (Dunn, 2014). Managers in social care have a perception that workers are much less digitally skilled than workers' perception of their own digital knowledge and skills; for example, whereas 97% of staff felt confident about their basic online skills only 48%

Table 4.1: Use of social media platforms by practitioners to contact or communicate with service users

Question: Do you use, or have you used, any of the following platforms to contact and/or communicate with service users? (please tick all boxes that are relevant to you)

	To contact and connect with service users (%)	To respond to service users but only after contact from service user (%)	Not helpful (%)	Not appropriate (%)
WhatsApp	18.29	4.10	34.36	50.09
Skype	17.18	2.35	47.20	17.18
Facetime	2.87	0.96	38.89	59.20
Other instant/ private messaging	3.27	1.64	22.49	73.62
Facebook	5.23	1.44	15.32	79.28
Twitter	2.81	0.94	19.49	86.70
LinkedIn	1.35	0.77	6.76	91.51

Source: Buzzi, 2020

of managers thought their staff had the basic online skills they needed; 91% of staff felt confident about their awareness of basic online security, while only 40% of managers thought the same of their staff; and, although 89% of staff felt confident about their information literacy skills, only 27% of managers thought that their staff had the confidence and information literacy skills they needed. This difference in perception could potentially lead to an imbalance in how digital and social media technologies are used in social work practice in order to better support people who access services and to meet their needs (Dunn, 2014; Buzzi, 2020).

The increasing digital divide and the challenge of digital exclusion highlight the need for assessment of digital access and digital enablement as part of social work assessments. This also underscores the need for appropriate training so that social work and social care practitioners can develop the necessary knowledge, skills and capabilities required for supporting and safeguarding people who access services both online and offline.

Underpinning the 'social' in health and social care

'Health is created and lived by people within the settings of their everyday life; where they learn, work, play, and love.' This well-known dictum from the Ottawa Charter published by the World Health Organization (WHO, 1986), which set the foundation for an ecological and situated approach to health, is as relevant in today's digital society as it was three decades ago. A situated approach considers the individual, physical, organisational and social context of people's lives as the objects of intervention (Poland et al, 2009).

In the last few decades we have seen an increasing recognition of and attention to more holistic health and the diversity of factors that influence people's health and wellbeing. This has consequently heightened the demand for integrated care and services and has increased the need for interagency and interprofessional working and collaboration between different services with diverse knowledge, disciplinary orientation, culture and priorities. Social media can support such an integration process by allowing greater and closer collaboration and coproduction among services and the ownership and proactive engagement of people who access services. However, this poses both opportunities and challenges.

Other than traditional prevention strategies directed toward individuals and their behaviour, the situated approach considers the setting, context and the systemic and socio-ecological factors that influence individuals' and communities' health and wellbeing. This recognises that health and wellbeing are embedded within structural and social systems that shape individual experience (Megele with Buzzi, 2017a; Megele and Buzzi, 2017b), including workplace and communities as well as the wider socio-ecological settings or special settings such as prisons; WHO's 'healthy setting' initiative is in recognition and a reflection of these dynamics (Green et al, 2000; Poland et al, 2009). The advent of social networks provides a new space where people meet, learn, work, play, love and develop (boyd and Ellison, 2007). This enables social media to cut across and influence all these settings and underpins the importance of social in health and social care (Megele with Buzzi, 2017a;

Buzzi and Megele, 2020); conversely, the 'social' in health and social care highlights the importance of access to and effective use of social media.

Social media, relationships and social capital

Much of our lives are passed in the company of others, and relationships lay the foundation of our experience (Megele, 2015). Embedded within these relationships are the 'social capital' – that is, the resources and support to engage in dynamics and structures of civil society and to promote and sustain one's relationships and social identity – that individuals can draw upon to meet their own needs. Individuals' social capital and relationships, and the patterns and dynamics of these, influence their ability, potential and opportunity for meeting their needs, securing goods and services, giving and receiving care and affection, and for learning, development and growth (Bourdieu, 1986; Putnam, 1995; Coleman, 1998; Field, 2005).

Pierre Bourdieu (1986) studied the patterns and dynamic of how the middle and upper classes used the material and human resources embedded in their social networks and relationships to meet their own needs and advance their own interest and position of advantage. Thinking of social capital as the power to enhance one's own position in a given context, Bourdieu (1986) saw a link between social capital and social inequalities.

The social augmentation hypothesis states that online social communication amplifies individuals' total social resources by providing an additional avenue for connection and interaction with others (Bessière et al, 2008).

The social nature of online posts in social networking sites offer considerable potential for keeping people connected and developing and maintaining their social networks and relationships.

Given its potential for communication and for developing and maintaining relationships with others, digital and social media technologies have become an important part of people's everyday lives. Individuals use a combination of resources and modalities to connect with others, including both synchronous (for example, voice or video calls or chatting) and asynchronous (for example, emails and social networking sites) connections. The increased ease, flexibility, efficiency and quality of online communication and connection play a critical role in supporting and enhancing social bonds and societal dynamics across the world. The augmentation hypothesis suggests that individuals use media to develop their social relationships (Walther, 1996; Megele, 2014) and that the use of social media supports and enhances users' existing social relationships (Valkenburg and Peter, 2009).

Such interactions with social media, even if purely online, have positive effects on people's sense of identity and wellbeing. For example, research indicates that when a medium such as a digital device (phone, tablet, computer or others) provides the user with social connection and feedback users tend to treat such a medium as if it is a social actor; this is true even in textual communication and in the absence of anthropomorphic figures (figures having human characteristics or similarity to human figure, for example androids, animation, avatars, and so on) (Reeves and Nass, 1996).

Despite the positive functions of media, however, the social use of media does not always benefit individual users. For example, in some cases, lonely individuals who go to media to mitigate social isolation may end up aggravating their social isolation (Kim et al, 2009). From the perspective of the displacement hypothesis, media use may consume a substantial amount of time sacrificing other valuable activities such as face-to-face communication without providing appropriate functions for facilitating social relations, thereby limiting actual social relations (Kraut et al, 1998; Nie, 2001; Putnam, 1995).

Digital storytelling as a tool for diversity and advocacy

Digital storytelling has gained recognition as an education and health promotion tool and is an emerging pathway for enhanced community health, offering the possibility for individuals, practitioners and communities to engage and exchange information in meaningful ways (Gubrium, 2009; Matthews and Sunderland, 2013). As an innovative tool for community health advocacy, digital storytelling offers possibilities to engage people of different cultural backgrounds and allows each individual and community to tell their own story and share their narrative of identity. This supports cultural promotion and cultural appreciation while promoting greater awareness and understanding of diversity and cultural needs of individuals and communities.

Merging storytelling customs with computer mediated communication is a powerful way to share information, knowledge and solutions to support individuals' and communities' health and wellbeing and provide social care in a culturally relevant and impactful manner. For example, merging storytelling with care for people living with Alzheimer's or dementia can enable learning about those challenges through everyday stories of people who experience them; at the same time, this can challenge stigma and share the cultural wisdom and preference of individuals and communities by evidencing how people care and expect to be cared for in a given culture and context.

Digital life storybooks are an example of digital storytelling that is used to support and enhance the sense of individual integrity and the quality of people's lives. Similar to traditional life storybooks, digital life storybooks follow a chronological order from childhood until the current time; for example, a digital life storybook can be divided into various segments such as: childhood, adolescence or teenage life, midlife, career, and so on until present time. However, digital life storybooks adopt a structured approach and use digital technologies to create a more dynamic and interactive life storybook.

Digital life storybooks might include visual material, such as photographs of significant others, family and friends, favourite places and activities, and so on. They may also include the person's favourite songs or music, video clips of movies or recorded events, accompanied by narration of significant events and quotations from the person or their partner or loved ones and so on. Digital storytelling and digital storybooks can be helpful in complementing and enhancing quality of life for older people and people who experience dementia or other challenges. For example, photographs, music, video and narration can be matched (such as playing a person's favourite dance music alongside photographs of them dancing with their partner) to rekindle memories and evoke emotions that were associated with those happy and/or significant moments in the person's life.

Social media and disability

New media offer a new context and language for communicating and connecting with others and for developing and maintaining relationships. Many of the affordances of new media are helpful for people with disabilities, autistic people, people experiencing mental health difficulties, and others.

For example, autistic people may find face-to-face in-person communication excessively stimulating; the abundance of online text communication offers an alternative way of relating to others without some of the stimulation, reaction and cognitive demand that are characteristic of face-to-face communication. Whereas face-to-face and video, and to an extent audio, encounters require attention to verbal and non-verbal cues and immediate interactive response (Burgoon and Hoobler, 2002), textual communication involves less self-disclosure and, therefore, lower attention and scrutiny from others. As a result, users of text-based communication have less stimuli and better control over the conversation. For example, they can better pace the conversation with longer and more flexible reaction time to suit their needs. Text-based communication also allows its users to distance themselves from their actions and social media interactions and to maintain greater focus on self and own intentions (McKenna, 2007; Megele, 2014). This offers a new alternative channel of communication that people with autism may prefer. This challenges and alters the dominant and taken-for-granted assumption that face-to-face communication presents the ideal form of conversation, and opens the door for a new world of multitasking and texting, and mediated conversations without verbal and non-verbal complexities (see Megele, 2014; Buzzi and Megele, 2020). Living with autism may have many different meanings and significance for different people: however, living with autism provides an example of how interpersonal relations can be mediated by technology in an effective and constructive manner to suit individual needs and preferences on a more person-centred basis.

Example: Using Facebook for support

In this lived example, used with permission, Facebook has become a key tool in all aspects of life for an older person living with dementia, without the older person needing to understand how Facebook works.

> Dad had dementia but with a daily visit from us and attendance at a lunch club, he was getting by until he broke his hip. After about eight weeks in hospital and rehab he came home and was assessed as needing four short visits a day. This was contracted through an agency with him paying.
>
> The first time he was left alone in the house he tried to go out with his walking frame and tried to cross a very busy road. It was then that I realised I needed someone to be with him throughout the day urgently. Using my Facebook account I posted my status as – "Can anyone come and help me look after my dad for the next few days – I will pay you". Two of my friends offered.
>
> The agency supporting dad could be variable in quality so I stopped using them, found a day centre (using the internet as he was a self funder so adult services now had no involvement) he could go to four days a week and between my two Facebook friends, and another lady who was one of their friends, me and my husband and the woman who had been dad's cleaner covered the whole week. Taking him out and about and doing things like helping him cook a meal for both of us.
>
> At this point I set up a Facebook group called 'dad cover' and each month I posted up a list of the times we needed care for the following month. The three lasses who use Facebook would reply to say which times they wanted and I would confirm it back. If anyone needed to change a shift they could post there and see if someone else could do it rather than me having to get it covered.

We also used it to share hints and tips about looking after dad and his house and to update each other on what he had done so people knew whether he might be tired or if he had particularly enjoyed something. Typical messages covered things like, "I made some veggie soup – it will need eating by Thursday." "Does anyone know where dad's metal framed glasses were last seen?" and, "Here's a link to the NHS choices page on cellulitis." Things that I actually felt would be waste of time to write down every day, but that when they needed to know they could post a message and say it. We also used it to share photos of bruises, sores so that the relevant health professionals could be shown them.

We never had a care plan or a risk assessment. People's brief was "make dad as happy and active as you can. Do whatever you would do if he was your dad."

It was also really useful for posting pictures or video of what we were doing with dad so that the following day we could use it with him to remind him and as a topic of conversation. This was particularly useful if he needed to wait for something (for example, at the hospital) where he could get quite frustrated and distressed. Being able to distract him with pictures or video of what he has been up to was very handy. Also useful in those situations are 'Google images' (typing in fire engines or fire stations – his former job) or YouTube (footage of fires so he can critique the firefighters' technique, or of World War two (he was in the RAF then).

We additionally used it to discuss the employment status of the people involved. We shared links and consulted the HMRC website and decided they were all self-employed.

This worked for over two years by which time dad needed someone with him overnight so we moved so he could move in with us. We continued using the group so that people could look after dad for some evening and weekends to allow us to do things with our kids. Again using the group meant I could keep everyone up to date with one message, that I could monitor and update things while away from him with work. When people arrived to look after dad we could get on with being 'respited' without spending half an hour telling them stuff.

In the last six months for various reasons we have changed to be only using two lasses and I am now using an agency more. We noted that when they take dad out he was telling them he couldn't walk and needed a wheelchair. We were able to video dad walking round the supermarket and using the self-service checkout. We put the video on Facebook so that they can show that to dad when they go out to reassure him that he can walk with a trolley."

The family carer in this example shows how social media can be used not only to connect people but as a tool to manage someone's care and support. Using Facebook as the individuals care plan and communication plan between the team and the family made it possible for a fluid and flexible approach to meeting dad's needs. In this case, the Facebook group provided a shared space that served as the point of reference for everyone involved. Such a single point of reference ensured continuity and allowed for effective and clear communication between different carers and the family. While Facebook may have had little meaning to the person being supported, it enabled the family and those supporting him to share stories and also to remind him about what he himself could and could not do.

For social work and social care practice the example of using Facebook demonstrates that, with a bit of imagination, social media can be used as a way of connecting people and communities and building community capacity. It also highlights that resolving problems and building capacity often does not need complex or bespoke digital tools and resources. If people are digitally literate and social media enabled, in all likelihood, it is possible to solve, or at least better support, their care and support issues collaboratively and effectively using the available means at hand. Having said that, it is important to note the need for reflection and careful consideration of the ethical implications of such arrangements to ensure awareness and respect for individual dignity and integrity at all times. It is also worth mentioning that given the intimate nature of some of the photos (for example, photos of bruises and sores), as long as the person has capacity for consent, it is important that they are consulted and have the opportunity to give or deny consent for taking and sharing such intimate photos and information. In this manner, families, carers and practitioners can ensure that people's care is in line with their preferences and values, and respects their rights, integrity, self-esteem and dignity.

Social media and apps

The example of using Facebook highlights how basic social media functionalities (in this case a Facebook group) can be used to coordinate and meet the needs of an older adult with complex needs. Many of the functionalities offered by the Facebook group in the example and the manner in which it was used can be supported by various apps. There is an abundance of apps for supporting adults with various needs. Three examples of apps that may be helpful for supporting adults who access services follow:

- Myhomehelper is an app for older adults and provides calendar, reminders, diary, news, photos and video calling. By combining helpful reminders with clock and calendar as well as photos (for example, family photos) and news, it offers a simple interface that is helpful and supportive of the caring process. The messages and reminders can help reduce carer burden, provide reassurance for the individual and offer memory stimulation as well as reminiscence.
- RallyRound aims to help people to live independently in their own homes for longer, support carers, and reduce social isolation. It offers a series of functionalities including providing performance data and the possibility to networks and enhance people's social capital. Using this app, family members, friends, volunteers and professional can create support networks (teams) within the app to organise and provide practical help for people who access services and their carers.
- Nourish offers a mobile working framework which aims to support care providers in delivery of an integrated care

solution. It takes account of informal carers and aims to engage such carers. It also offers integration of health and social care information on a per-person/individual basis. This is more of a planning software that allows for different information for an individual to be entered into and managed by the app.

Conclusion

People's needs are complex and require effective coordination and seamless collaboration between services in order to offer an integrated service that meets the needs of individuals and communities. Key components and prerequisites for such integration are effective and timely sharing of information and coordination mechanisms; social media offers an ideal medium and conduit for information sharing and coproduction of services. Indeed, the internet and associated new media offer new possibilities and opportunities for adults and older people as well as people with disabilities, and those with different information processing capabilities, social or relational preferences, and/or physical or mental health difficulties (Ellis and Kent, 2011; Haller, 2010). These affordances offer unprecedented opportunities for challenging stigma and supporting people who access services. What is needed is that practitioners maintain an open and inquiring mind to explore and creatively provide person-centred solutions that maximise choice, individual autonomy and control while meeting people's needs and ensuring their safety and wellbeing in line with their own values and preferences. In order to do this social work and social care practitioners need to consider some of the following points.

The main practice learning points from this chapter for social workers can be summarised as follows:

- Challenge the social stereotypes and stigma about and affecting the people who access services and their practice; these include claims about older adults and their use of digital and social media technologies, stigma and stereotypes about ageing, disability, autism, dementia, mental health and other challenges affecting adults who access services.

- Tap into the power of social media and use social media and digital storytelling to promote diversity as well as alternative and preferred narratives of vulnerability and identity to refine and redefine these with a focus on empowerment and appreciation of individuals' uniqueness and capabilities.
- Develop a nuanced understanding of intersectionality and adults' experiences and uses of social media as well as barriers to access to the internet or digital technologies to enable and empower adults of all ages so that they can access and use the wealth of online information and resources to enhance their knowledge, make informed decisions and meet their own needs.
- Have a situated understanding of health and social care and how social media have accentuated and raised the importance of the social in health and care.
- Furthermore, to ensure that adult social work practitioners are able to operate in a professional manner and support people who access services both online and offline, adult social workers should:
  - Enhance their own understanding of digital and social media technologies and develop their new media literacies and ability to use social media effectively and professionally in practice.
  - Understand the differences between online and offline environments, communication, behaviours and identities and their implications for practice.
  - Enhance their ethical and professional knowledge and ability and their understanding of e-professionalism.
  - Develop their digital knowledge, skills and capabilities and ability to assess online risks and opportunities, support well-being and ensure holistic safeguarding of people who access services.
  - Be able to capitalise on use of social media to combat loneliness and enhance people's social networks and social capital.

References

Bessière, K., Kiesler, S., Kraut, R. and Boneva, B. (2008) 'Effects of internet use and social resources in changes in depression', *Information, Communication and Society*, 11(1): 47–70.

Bourdieu, P. (1986) 'The forms of capital', in J. G. Richardson (ed) *The Handbook of Theory and Research for Sociology of Education*. New York: Greenwood, pp 241–58.

boyd, d. and Ellison, N. (2007) 'Social networking sites: Definition, history, and scholarship', *Journal of Computer-Mediated Communication*, 13(1): 210–30.

Burgoon, J. and Hoobler, G. (2002) 'Nonverbal signals', in M. L. Knapp and J. A. Daly (eds), *Handbook of Interpersonal Communication* (3rd edn). Thousand Oaks, CA: Sage, pp 240–99.

Buzzi, P. (2020) *Relationship based Practice in Digital Age*. London: PSW Network.

Buzzi, P. and Megele, C. (2020) *Digital Practice and Working with Children and Young People Online*. London: PSW Network.

Coleman, J. S. (1998) *Foundations of Social Theory*. Cambridge, MA: Belknap Press.

Dunn, S. (2014) *Digital Capabilities in Social Care*. Leeds: Skills for Care.

Ellis, K. and Kent, M. (2011) *Disability and New Media. Routledge Studies in New Media and Cyberculture*. New York: Routledge.

Field, J. (2005) *Social Capital and Lifelong Learning*. Bristol: Policy Press.

Green, L. W., Poland, B. D. and Rootman, I. (2000) 'The settings approach to health promotion', in B. D. Poland, L. W. Green and I. Rootman (eds) *Settings for Health Promotion: Linking Theory and Practice*, Thousand Oaks, CA: Sage, pp. 1–43.

Gubrium. A. (2009) 'Digital storytelling as a method for engaged scholarship in anthropology', *Practicing Anthropology*, Fall, 31(4): 5–9. doi: http://dx.doi.org/10.17730/praa.31.4.6n60q02x710l6477

Haller, B. (2010) *Representing Disability in an Ableist World: Essays on mass media*. Louisville, KY: The Avocado Press.

Jones, C. and Shao, B. (2011) 'The net generation and digital natives, implications for higher education: A literature review commissioned by the Higher Education Academy'. Available at: https://www.heacademy.ac.uk/system/files/next-generation-and-digital-natives.pdf

Kim, J., LaRose, R. and Peng, W. (2009) 'Loneliness as the cause and the effect of problematic Internet use: The relationship between Internet use and psychological well-being', *Cyberpsychology & Behavior*, 12(4): 451–5.

Kraut, R., Patterson, M., Lundmark, V., Kiesler, S., Mukopadhyay, T. and Scherlis, W. (1998) 'Internet paradox: A social technology that reduces social involvement and psychological well-being?', *American Psychologist*, 53(9): 1017–31.

Madden, M. and Zickuhr, K. (2011) '65% of online adults use social networking sites'. Pew Research Center, Internet and Technology. Available at: http://www.pewinternet.org/2011/08/26/65-of-online-adults-use-social-networking-sites/

Matthews, N. and Sunderland, N. (2013) 'Digital life-story narratives as data for policy makers and practitioners: thinking through methodologies for large-scale multimedia qualitative datasets', *Journal of Broadcasting and Electronic Media*, 57(1): 97–114.

McKenna, K. Y. A. (2007) 'Through the Internet looking glass: Expressing and validating the true self', In A. Joinson, K. Y. A. McKenna, T. Postmes and U.-D. Reips (eds), *The Oxford Handbook of Psychology* (pp 205–22). New York: Oxford University Press.

Megele C. with Buzzi, P. (2017a) *Safeguarding Children and Young People Online*. Bristol: Policy Press.

Megele, C. and Buzzi P. (2017b) *Learning Through Observation: A bio-psychosocial and developmental perspective*. Abingdon: Routledge.

Megele, C. (2014) 'Theorizing Twitter chat', *Journal of Perspectives in Applied Academic Practice*, 2(2). Available at: http://jpaap.napier.ac.uk/index.php/JPAAP/article/view/106/html

Megele, C. (2015) *Psychosocial and Relationship Based Practice*. London: Critical Publishing.

Nie, N. H. (2001) 'Sociability, interpersonal relations, and the Internet: Reconciling conflicting findings', *American Behavioral Scientist*, 45: 420–35.

Ofcom (2019) *Children's Media Use and Attitudes*. Available at: https://www.ofcom.org.uk/research-and-data/media-literacy-research/childrens

Poland, B., Krupa, G. and McCall, D. (2009) 'Settings for health promotion: an analytic framework to guide intervention design and implementation', *Health Promotion Practice*, 10(4): 505–16.

Portsmouth News (2017) 'Hampshire council to use Amazon Echo technology for elderly social care patients' (26 August 2017). Available at: https://www.portsmouth.co.uk/news/hampshire-council-to-use-amazon-echo-technology-for-elderly-social-care-patients-1-8122146

Prensky, M. (2001) 'Digital natives, digital immigrants', *On the Horizon*, Vol 9, pp 1–6.

Putnam, R. D. (1995) 'Bowling alone: America's declining social capital', *Journal of Democracy*, 6(1): 65–78.

Reeves, B. and Nass, C. (1996) *The Media Equation: How people treat computers, television, and new media like real people and places.* New York: Cambridge University Press.

Pew Research Center (2017) *Technology Use Among Seniors.* Pew Research Center. Available at: http://www.pewinternet.org/2017/05/17/technology-use-among-seniors/

Selwyn, N. (2009) 'The digital native: myth and reality', *Aslib Proceedings*, 61: 364-79.

Valkenburg, P. and Peter, J. (2009) 'Social consequences of the internet for adolescents', *Current Directions in Psychological Science*, 18(1): 1–5.

Walther, J. B. (1996) 'Computer-mediated communication impersonal, interpersonal, and hyperpersonal interaction', *Communication Research*, 23: 3–43.

WHO (1986) *The Ottawa Charter for Health Promotion.* World Health Organization. Available at: http://www.who.int/healthpromotion/conferences/previous/ottawa/en/

Zickuhr, K. and Smith, A. (2012) *Digital Differences.* Pew Research Center, Internet and Technology. Available at: http:www.pewinternet.org/2012/04/13/digital-differences/

5

Social media and mental health social work

Ruth Allen and Peter Buzzi

Social media: our modern social and emotional environment

The relationship between social media and mental health is often dominated by a discourse of risk and negative outcomes. From the mental health consequences of 'overuse' of social media (Pantic et al, 2012), to the potential psychological and emotional consequences of 'cyberbullying' and 'trolling' of adults and children and young people, to the risks associated with online sites that promote self-harm or suicide (*Guardian*, 2014; Jenaro, 2018; Popovac, 2017) or other forms of abuse (Kloess et al, 2014), debates around the risks of harm associated with social media are widespread in popular culture and by politicians and often overlook its potential benefits.

Much academic research into online and social media activity has also tended to focus on the risks of negative impacts on mental wellbeing. This includes the suggestion that internet and social media communications reduce face-to-face interactions, causing isolation and vulnerability to online abuse and predators, and increasing levels of loneliness (Primack et al, 2017; Yao and Zhong, 2014).

However, as research in this field develops, more recent studies suggest that interactive social media and online resources have mixed effects (for a brief overview of research in respect of adolescents see Durbin et al, 2018), highlighting potential benefits as well as negative outcomes. Studies indicate that impact and experiences depend on many factors, including the nature and patterns of usage, specific online content, the pre-existing mental health and wellbeing of the individual, psychological factors and the meanings associated with online interactions, and the degree to which people can control their experience and communications with others.

Social media plays an important role in everyday communication and social relationships and is a growing feature of social work and mental health practice. Therefore, as in all areas of practice, social workers in mental health need to be open-minded and reflective about social media and its impact and should develop their knowledge in this area and use it effectively in the complexities of their work. The British Association of Social Workers (BASW) provides ethical and practice guidance for all social workers on social media (BASW, 2018) to support this.

This chapter will first focus on some of the evidence of benefits of social media and online resources relevant to the field of mental health and social work. It will then explore some of the specific risks that social workers in mental health contexts need to understand, manage and hold in balance. The chapter concludes with some recommendations for mental health social work.

The positive opportunities of social networks

Social workers in mental health fulfil a variety of roles (Allen, 2014). These include: promoting personalised social care and determining eligibility for statutory resources; promoting social inclusion and recovery through rights, citizenships and relationship-based practice; supporting and protecting families, groups and communities; and, protecting human rights through application of legal powers such as the Mental Health Act and Mental Capacity Act. Social media may be relevant to all of these social work roles, but it is particularly relevant to social work's role in promoting recovery, tackling stigma, discrimination and societal exclusion (material, economic, educational, social or cultural), and increasing social capital and connections.

Social capital is the sum of resources, actual or potential, that accrue to a person or group from access to a network of relationships or membership in a group (Bourdieu, 1997). Greater advantageous social capital increases capability to mobilise these resources – that is, to function socially, have agency and give and take support effectively in groups, communities and in social, political and culture milieux.

When people experience mental health problems, they also frequently experience relationship strains and shrinkage in their social networks. This often worsens and can elongate the effects of mental distress and the source of difficulties in the first place. This increases the chance of loneliness, isolation, alienation and a wide range of other negative outcomes affecting the person's health, wellbeing and material resources.

With the extraordinary growth in usage of Facebook, Twitter, LinkedIn, Instagram, Snapchat and a vast number of other social media apps and interactive forums, our understanding of fundamental concepts such as community, sociality, loneliness, connectedness, friendship and relationships is also changing. This changes the social context within which social workers operate and, therefore, social workers must understand and work with the new possibilities for social connectedness arising from these changes and the changing online relationships. Digital and online experiences have changed significantly from primarily one-way broadcast and 'information receipt' or one-on-one exchanges, to an environment of dynamic and expanding relationships and networks of information exchange.

Recent studies suggest both mainstream and mental-health-specific online networking and social media use are likely to enhance positive social behaviour in both the online and offline worlds. For instance, the findings of the Australian Psychological Society's online survey (Mathews and Cameron, 2010) of the use of social networking sites by 1834 adults aged 18–80 years showed that people both developed new ways of relating and enhanced pre-existing relationships, as well as forging new ones through social networking and social media. In other words, social media and online networks enhanced the sum total of social connections both online and offline, and mostly in positive ways.

This perspective is consistent with recent developments in social network theory which implies that the more a person socialises in a traditional sense, the more they will socialise online (Mathews and Cameron, 2010) and vice versa. Other studies have also indicated that social networking has a positive impact on social connectedness and wellbeing (Valkenburg and Peter, 2009) and other studies suggest there may be benefits for those who find face-to-face contact difficult, such as those who are shy or introverted (Wolfradt and Doll, 2001). This can operate at local as well as community, national and international levels. It is highly relevant to current and emerging directions in community and social network focused developments in social work practice in mental health. Two examples of such an approach include the NHS Open Dialogue (NHS, ongoing) and Webber et al (2018) studies into wellbeing benefit and the social workers' role in 'Connecting People' within their families and communities. This approach uses social network theory to develop skills and replicable ways of enhancing people's social capital, wellbeing and mental health within geographical localities. Social media and online connectivity extends options and augments the human- and place-based services and relational skills base of social work models.

Social media as mediated reflective space

For a wide variety of reasons, people who may benefit from mental health support and services may at times be unwilling to seek help or engage early with mental health services. Many continue without the appropriate support until they face a crisis or more severe problems. Positive social media can offer platforms for such individuals to engage in communities of interest (such as described in Chapter 7) and encourage seeking help and engaging with formal support and services.

Evidence suggests individuals with serious mental ill health are in fact more likely to share their thoughts, feelings, and personal experiences and views through online media and blogging, and to establish online friendships on social media sites than people without mental ill health; they are also more likely to search and access health information online. This could be due to the dissociative effect of online posting and a perception of social media as a non-threatening medium that offers avenues for different forms of self-expression, including anonymously, and opportunities for connecting, conversing and interacting with other individuals within the safety of one's own home. This shows the importance and potential for online support for people experiencing mental ill health.

Social media has created a new discursive space that offers everyone the voice and the space to tell their stories in YouTube videos, blogs, tweets, Facebook posts, likes, Diggs, images and infographics and so on. This can be part of transforming conversations from hierarchical 'expert to patient' consultations to collaborative formulations between professionals and experts by experience. This is further supported and accelerated by communities of interest such as Big White Wall, Black Dog, and Mental Health Chat (@MHChat) which provide a shared, validating and non-judgemental space for all. Such online communities offer peer support and allow individuals to relate to one another based on shared experiences and to create a sense of belonging to a supportive community. Such community members can find others with shared experience of mental ill health, generating a sense of acceptance which in turn mitigates isolation and stigma and encourages and facilitates help seeking on their own terms.

> Today's patients have access to significant new resources. Not those controlled by the system, but those created by patients themselves: the forum, the voice in the night from the other side of the world saying 'have you tried this?' and, increasingly, the ability to share your bio-data and your life experiences with your community of fellow sufferers.
>
> These new resources are created by the lower transaction costs of the loosely coupled, but intelligently communicating, crowd of 'people like

> me'. This is not 'coproduction' – which is what those people called patients are still supposed to do to help the system. It's much more like hacking healthcare from the bottom up, from the outside. (Hodgkin, 2015)

Social media, civic engagement and mental health

'Social capital' has also been defined as having the resources to engage in more formal structures of civil society, sustaining civic identity through reciprocity and norms of cooperation and trust within communities and societies (Putnam, 2000). In this definition, social capital includes access to the processes of political democracy and enfranchisement of citizens.

According to the United Nations (UN), a citizenship and human rights approach to mental health is crucial to transform experiences of mental health difficulties and their associated challenges and misunderstandings across the world.

Dainius Puras, UN Special Rapporteur on the right to health, in his 2017 report on mental health to the Human Rights Council in Geneva condemned the neglect of what he calls 'the preconditions of poor mental health', including violence, disempowerment, social exclusion, and harmful conditions at work and school' and advocated that:

> The crisis in mental health should be managed not as a crisis of individual conditions, but as a crisis of social obstacles which hinders individual rights. Mental health policies should address the 'power imbalance' rather than 'chemical imbalance'. (Puras, 2017)

The power of social media to mobilise people en masse behind political and social causes has become undeniable. While 'unaccountable' claims and 'fake news' in social media political campaigning and commercial activity have raised many concerns (Vosoughi et al, 2018), positive mobilisation by advocates for mental health, equality and human rights has drawn people together in communities of interest in politics and in mental health. This is playing a major part in reducing stigma and promoting mental health awareness and literacy as well as increased civic connectedness for people experiencing mental health problems and their allies and advocates of social inclusion and rights (Globalwebindex, 2017).

Social workers have a key role in ensuring people can access their civic and citizenship rights. Being part of social media and social networking communities, sharing and receiving information and building relationships with other people, can be an important part of this role; being connected with society and ensuring a platform for expression and open contribution toward equality and better opportunities for people we work with are essential effective and empowering social work and mental health practice.

Mental health, e-interventions and health intervention technologies

An important area for social work practice is the understanding of the targeted use of technology for mental health support and intervention. 'Health information technologies' refer to the technologies that make use of the internet and apps, text messaging protocols and other similar channels to deliver telehealth and telepsychiatry services. These apps have numerous uses and far-reaching effects. For example, health intervention technologies can support, complement and enhance mental health services provided by professionals and primary care practitioners who may often lack the training, support and time to provide full-service mental health care for people requiring or using mental health services. These technologies enable the practitioners to use telemedicine consultation with remote specialists for support and guidance in relation to complex decisions and diagnosis or complex situations or before providing specific care components. The area of virtual consultation and virtual intervention is a developing and expanding area for telehealth, telepsychiatry and teleconsultation that offer a range of interventions and clinical decision support tools and services.

These technologies offer an avenue for complementing and bringing specialists, services and care to areas where there is a shortage of such expertise or services. For example, health intervention technologies have been invaluable in delivering mental health support and interventions for survivors of natural disasters or other large-scale disasters who experienced mental health difficulties or crisis. In such situations, virtual interventions can be scaled based on needs and can provide rapid response, including initial evaluation and triage as well as specific mental health support or intervention. This can complement on the ground and face-to-face work and can cover a large number of people much more efficiently and quickly than before. In fact, tele-interventions and health intervention technologies have been used successfully for a number of catastrophes ranging from the tsunami in Asia to Hurricane Katrina in the US.

Telepsychiatry, tele-interventions and health intervention technologies can also be used in the area of prevention. Most mental health care has been focused on crisis intervention and 'treatment' and traditionally local authorities have focused on severe cases of mental ill health only. However, creative use of social media and tele-interventions and other health intervention technologies offer great opportunities for preventive service and mental health promotion and prevention of mental ill health. In fact, given that preventive interventions are usually of lower intensity and lower complexity, they lend themselves to the lower complexity of tele-interventions and health intervention technologies.

Mental health apps and avatar therapy

A vast variety of platforms, apps and online tools are used in mental health to provide intervention, support and therapy for people who experience mental health difficulties. An example is the use of avatar therapy for people experiencing psychosis.

The introduction of antipsychotic medication helped many people experiencing psychosis and resulted in wave of discharges from psychiatric hospitals. However, aside from its side effects, unfortunately, one in four people with schizophrenia do not respond to antipsychotic medication and continue to experience persistent auditory hallucinations. These hallucinations have a huge impact on people's everyday lives and result in significant persecutory experiences that can lead to suicide.

Digital technologies and virtual reality allow for the creation of avatars and the possibility to manipulate facial expressions; this allows more natural facial expressions that can communicate emotions. It also allows and stimulates social interactions in a controlled and yet dynamic and more naturalistic environment. The combination of these capabilities allows the creation of more naturalistic avatars. The use of avatar therapy offers a new relational intervention that draws on a number of different disciplines and therapeutic theories and approaches to intervene, support, educate, and give people greater control over their thoughts and emotions. For example, in cases of psychosis and schizophrenia avatar therapy helps people gain greater control over their 'voices'. Another example includes the use of virtual reality for treatment of various types of phobia (for example agoraphobia, claustrophobia and acrophobia). In these cases, using virtual reality the individual is supported to gradually explore and experience virtually the elements and circumstances that trigger their fears and in a safe and controlled manner while being supported in the process.

Research indicates strong correlation between early life trauma experienced by children of neglectful or abusive parents and the development of mental ill health in later life, including hearing voices and other auditory hallucinations. The experience of persecutory auditory hallucinations can be conceptualised as an exteriorisation of the 'persecutory parent' or the persecutory and critical component of the psyche that cannot be tolerated by the self (Buzzi, 2020). Therefore, in this case, avatar therapy aims to help individuals experiencing auditory hallucination to gain control over their externalised part of psyche and to reintegrate it within the self.

Hence, without engaging in clinical practice or recommending or prescribing medication or a given treatment or approach, knowledge of available therapies and support apps can provide social workers with a better understanding of the dynamics of mental ill health and additional resources in supporting people who access services. Furthermore, use of such resources and better awareness and understanding of mental ill health can enhance practice while helping prevent or challenge and change misconception around mental health. For example, people hearing voices are often advised to ignore the voices they hear and not to engage with them. However, research indicates that encouraging people who hear voices to enter into a dialogue with the voices they hear can have therapeutic effects. For more detailed discussion of avatar therapy and its use, see Buzzi and Megele (2020).

Social media and inequalities

There are a vast number of online resources providing support for mental wellbeing as well as resources for people with mental ill health. These range from informal online mental wellbeing communities and peer support to teleconsultation, telepsychiatry and online counselling. But not everyone uses or has access to the internet and social media, particularly in older age groups – although there is growing evidence of widening use throughout the age spectrum. As with all technologies, inequalities are spread across the population, between those with the resources and knowledge to use multiple social media platforms beneficially – potentially increasing their knowledge and social capital yet further every day – to those with no access to the technology and no knowledge of the potential benefits and deep well of useful information available.

For social workers, enabling access to good social media opportunities may be as important from an equalities perspective as overcoming poor access to education, work support, and recreational activities. Addressing equitable access to social media and online sources of support should increasingly be part of social work and the provision of funding to eligible adults and young people.

Where social workers are part of providing access to social media, this should be more than simply providing a digital device or an internet connection for service users. Support should include education in how to use online resources effectively and safely to enhance social connections, wellbeing and other desired outcomes. Ongoing dialogue about the benefits or issues arising from online relationships and experiences should be embedded in social workers' conversations with people, and on a par with conversations about offline and face-to-face relationships.

Evaluating risks and opportunities in mental health practice

Choice-making about boundaries, risks and relationships online is not intrinsically different for people who experience mental health difficulties. But the challenge of choosing and learning how to use social media platforms well may be amplified by the nature or severity of a person's mental health difficulties at a particular point in time. Social media poses a myriad of options, privacy and online profile choices, judgements about new social connections and risks of unwelcomed or abusive contacts. A person's mental capacity to make good judgements about social media usage – as in all aspects of their lives – will always be a professional concern for social workers.

Social workers should be skilled, non-prejudiced and knowledgeable to explore proportionately whether a person is able to make beneficial choices for themselves online and whether any aspect of the social media use and interface with others can result in negative, distressing or delusional experiences, or be seen as exploitative. As in all fields of practice, social workers in mental health support, protect and enable people within their social and environmental contexts. Therefore, practitioners need to be knowledgeable about those environments and contexts, both online and offline, and need to understand the cultural and affective importance of social media, virtual reality and evolving technology for people's lives and identities.

These questions need to be asked not just in respect of individuals using services, but also of their family and social network environments. It may be particularly relevant within families where an adult and/or parent is identified as having mental health problems and there is also a child or young person, perhaps acting as a young carer. Given the immersion of children and younger people within social media and its peer-group normalisation, their use of online and social media resources may be hugely important as a source of support and information. The great benefits of tailored online support for young people with siblings with mental health problems have been particularly explored through the 'e-sibling' action research project, for instance, which has successfully provided an online resource for siblings of people with psychosis (Sin et al, 2008).

At the community level (whether this means a material geographical community or an online, virtual community) too, social workers in mental health need to understand the role of social media, for instance, how service users and others in the geographical area use platforms such as Twitter or a local wiki to collaborate and connect over issues of local importance and meaning.

Safeguarding and social media in mental health

While the positives of social media and online support have been well described here, there are also significant risks of negative outcomes; social workers need to be aware of such risks and alert to their effects. It is essential that practitioners have a curious and open approach to social media for the very reason that such an approach offers a way into understanding the risks people may encounter. This includes the risk of social media experiences becoming integrated harmfully into negative belief systems, delusional or psychotic thoughts, obsessional behaviours or through re-experiencing trauma or other harm.

There may be risks for the person using mental health and social work services, or for others if the person using services is the perpetrator of harm. Social media risks of cyberbullying, trolling, stalking, grooming for sexual abuse or other criminal harm are ever-present in virtual worlds. Their impact on a person who experiences mental health difficulties, and potentially a range of additional problems, may be significantly amplified. If the social worker is unfamiliar with these risks, the conversation with service users to expose and address them may not happen.

A specific concern in adult mental health and children's services currently is the risk of 'radicalisation' from extremist groups – whether political, religious, cultish or others (HM Government, 2018). Evidence suggests these risks can be particularly promulgated online and such involvements can be covert and highly secretive if the person so wishes. The responsibility of public bodies working with people within health and social care services is to recognise early the risks of approach from exploitative groups and individuals, which in the early stages can include quite subtle early processes of 'grooming' and appealing to the isolation and disaffection that people may be feeling.

Evaluating these types of risk may involve working closely with people and their family and friends to understand the pattern and frequency of a person's social media usage if information from a service user is not forthcoming or to supplement the information they offer. Social media usage may be shared within members of a family so, within the provisions of confidentiality and information sharing policies, working effectively with a person's social network to understand their social media and online usage too may be key to identifying risks. The SMART mapping tool in Chapter 2 provides an interactive tool to discuss and identify people's social media presence and its risks and benefits.

Collaboration and coproduction through social media

Social work's role in mental health is often to challenge the power imbalances in services that vest expertise, solutions and understanding wholly or dominantly in professionals. Creating approaches that enable people to be the authors of their own recovery, on their own terms as much as possible, is a driving force for change in mental health and social care systems and service user movements. Social media and related online platforms offer rich opportunities for enhancing coproduction between service leaders, practitioners and people using social work and mental health services (Daneshvar et al, 2018; Repper and Perkins, 2009).

Use of social media to enhance coproduction also includes especially designed apps that enable direct communications between practitioners and service users or their families, for instance enabling self-management of triggers and signs of mental health deterioration and the sharing of information with professionals. These include communications via mobile devices about mood changes and self-management, and the use of an online social media support community hosted in a partnership between a health providers and self-help organisation.

Social media can create relationships that cut through formal power and status hierarchies in ways that go beyond the mental health experience, expanding social capital, social connections and knowledge transfer. An example of such an approach in the UK was the emergence of 'Social Care Curry' (SCC). This was an informal, inexpensive, unfunded meet-up in 2013 between people involved in providing, developing and using social care services, hosted in cities across England (and a few internationally). Another example was the Social Work and Media (Twitter handle: @SWSCMedia) network which started in 2011, creating an online community of practitioners, local authorities, service providers, academics, charities and people who access social care services with blogs, discussions, and Twitter chats that explored topical issues and promoted exchange of ideas and a better understanding of social work and social care practice and its complexities. Another example is Mental Health Chat (Twitter handle: @MHChat): launched on 1 February 2012, this is an open access online mental health community with about 90,000 members including professionals, academics, researchers and people with lived experience of mental health difficulties; the focus is challenging stigma, discussing and raising awareness of mental health issues and relevant topics, and supporting people who experience mental health difficulties. Indeed, Mental Health Chat (@MHChat) has been part of several national and international research projects to improve safeguarding and services for people who experience mental health difficulties. The hierarchy-flattening nature of these initiatives was a social media-driven approach to collaboration between social workers and social care leaders as well as other professionals, specialists and service users. One of the important aspects (and added value contribution) of these initiatives was in breaking down the boundaries of professional networks and being fully open to people with lived experience of their members and in particular in case of @MHChat for mental health services in an ethos of coproduction and equality.

Collaboration among social workers through social media

Social media is increasingly valuable in creating professional communities of interest, identity and collaborations. For social workers in mental health services in England, this has been particularly well developed through the success of social media (for example the 'Masked AMHP' closed Facebook group) and 'Google group' communities for Approved Mental Health Professionals (AMHPs) and, more recently, Best Interest Assessors (under the Mental Capacity Act 2005).

Social workers in mental health are often scattered across health-led services, frequently acting as sole practitioners in teams or in small numbers and carrying statutory responsibilities within autonomous decision-making frameworks. Online forums can offer professional support across geographical boundaries and can be used both in discursive and exploratory manners as well as responsive and informative ones, helping promote and develop good social work practice.

The delivery of services is becoming more diverse and, in many places, more fragmented. With increasing demand and workload, mental health social workers often have to work extended hours beyond a 9–5 working day and into evenings and weekends, depending on service needs and demands. This can be an obstacle for attending regular classroom training or keeping up to date as part of one's continuous professional development (CPD). Flexible e-learning courses and online CPD opportunities can bridge this gap and are more compatible with mental health social workers' commitments. Furthermore, the wealth of online information can provide mental health social workers with valuable resources and information, including the latest changes in legislation or developments in mental health social work. As funding for collaborative development opportunities (such as courses and conferences) are reduced and online learning becomes the norm, the ability and willingness of professionals to access and use online resources, information and forums effectively becomes more pressing. The use of online forums in mental health in England has become embedded in practice and has persisted, without external funding, for over five years, and continues to grow. It is an important model of success that meets and can adapt to contemporary professional and service needs.

Conclusion

The opportunities of social media and online resources in mental health are considerable and are beginning to be increasingly recognised and used in practice – this applies both to people using services and for professionals. The safeguarding, confidentiality and other risks of social media within the mental health sector need to be managed without losing sight of the benefits, and the inevitability that citizens with mental health needs will use new technologies available to all.

Social workers need to embrace social media and digital capabilities, developing and sustaining their knowledge and skills and being able to apply it to their particular work contexts. This is a fairly new area of capability and skills development for many social workers, but it is an area of growing importance. Therefore, learning about and maintaining contemporary knowledge in this area is essential for good social work practice in general and good mental health social work in particular.

Social workers enable choice and protect from harm, and their social media and professional online engagements and responsibilities should be in line with these objectives. The mental health social workers may find the following practice recommendations and examples helpful:

- Be aware of relational boundaries and maintain appropriate personal and professional boundaries and a balanced and healthy approach to online activities, taking into account one's own and others' strengths and vulnerabilities and how these may be amplified online or through experience of mental health difficulties. The SMART mapping tool described in Chapter 2 can be used as an interactive tool for self-reflection or in discussion with service users to explore and reflect upon the person's digital and social media presence and activities and associated risks and benefits.
- Be confident about exploring the benefits and risks that a particular individual (or a group) with specific mental health

difficulties or distress may experience in their interactions online (for example, whether the distress and isolation of agoraphobia is reduced through access to online communities for a particular person, or whether a person with obsessive compulsive behaviour is at risk of overusing social media to their detriment and worsening of distressing experiences in the long term). This requires the application of good mental health assessment, intersubjective and relationship-building skills to evaluate the person's online experience. For a more detailed discussion of online risks and online safeguarding see Buzzi and Megele (2020), which offers an evidence-informed risk typology for assessment of online risks and opportunities from a systemic perspective and for holistic (both online and offline) safeguarding of people who experience mental health difficulties.

- Support services users to optimise their ability to self-evaluate risks and benefits, which should be part of a recovery-focused, approach to the person themselves, maximising control and opportunities and reducing harms and distress.
- Enable people to explore the specific benefits of positive media platforms and websites focused on supporting mental health and wellbeing, including online self-help communities. These run on a continuum – from helping people access support groups and good information sites (such as MIND, Big White Wall, Black Dog, or Mental Health Chat) through to supporting people to make choices about online therapy offers. Social workers will often not be making the specific online therapy proposal, as this should be governed by the processes in place for any therapeutic offer and may come from another professional, but social workers may need both to assist people in making decisions about such resources and to work with multi-professional colleagues who may be developing such offers.
- Engage in the responsible use and development of online professional support and development communities and resources where relevant, such as those currently supporting AMHPs and BIAs, and professional use of Twitter and LinkedIn.
- Ensure adherence to the social media policies of national regulators and social work associations (for example, the

Social Work England standards and the BASW social media policy and the PSW best practice guidance on digital professionalism and online safeguarding).

References

Allen, R. (2014) *The Role of the Social Worker in Adult Mental Health Services*. London: The College of Social Work.

BASW (2018) 'BASW social media policy'. Available at: https://www.basw.co.uk/system/files/resources/Social%20Media%20Policy.pdf

Bourdieu, P. (1997) 'The forms of capital', in Halsey A.H., Lauder, H., Brown P. and Wells A.M. (eds) *Education, Culture, and Society*. Oxford: Oxford University Press, pp 46–58.

Buzzi, P. (2020) *Relationship based Practice in Digital Age*. London: PSW Network.

Buzzi, P. and Megele, C. (2020) *Digital Practice and Working With Children and Young People Online*. London: PSW Network.

Daneshvar, H., Anderson, S., Williams, R. and Mozaffar, H. (2018) 'How can social media lead to co-production (co-delivery) of new services for the elderly population? A qualitative study', *JMIR Human Factors*, 5(1).

Durbin, J., DeNapoles, C. and Lundeen, H. (2018) 'Social media and adolescents: what are the health risks?', *Clinical Advisor*. Available at: https://www.clinicaladvisor.com/home/features/social-media-and-adolescents-what-are-the-health-risks/2/

Globalwebindex (2017) '5 mental health campaigns that made a difference'. Available at: https://blog.globalwebindex.com/marketing/mental-health/

Guardian (2014) 'Number of children who are victims of cyberbullying doubles in a year', *The Guardian*. Available at: https://www.theguardian.com/society/2014/nov/14/35pc-children-teenagers-victims-cyberbullying-fears-grooming-tinder-snapchat

Hodgkin, P. (2015) 'Power to the people: signs off'. *Digitalhealth*. Available at: https://www.digitalhealth.net/2015/04/power-to-the-people-signs-off/

HM Government (2018) *Counter-terrorism Strategy (CONTEST)*. Available at: https://www.gov.uk/government/publications/counter-terrorism-strategy-contest-2018

Jenaro, C., Flores, N. and Frías, C. P. (2018) 'Systematic review of empirical studies on cyberbullying in adults: What we know and what we should investigate', *Aggression and Violent Behavior*, 38: 113–22.

Kloess, J. A., Beech, A. R. and Harkins, L. (2014) 'Online child sexual exploitation: Prevalence, process and offender characteristics', *Trauma, Violence and Abuse*, 15(2): 126–39.

Mathews, R. and Cameron, F. (2010) 'The social and psychological impact of online social networking', *APS National Psychology Week Survey InPsych*, 32(6).

NHS (ongoing) 'Open dialogue'. Available at: https://www.nelft.nhs.uk/aboutus-initiatives-opendialogue

Pantic, I., Damjanovic, A., Todorovic, J., Topalovic, D., Bojovic-Jovic, D., Ristic, S. and Pantic, S. (2012) 'Association between online social networking and depression in high school students: Behavioral physiology viewpoint', *Psychiatria Danubina*, 24: 90–3.

Popovac, M. (2017). *Beyond the School Gates: Experiences of cyberaggression and cyberbullying among adolescents in the UK*. Joint publication by the University of Buckingham and Sir John Cass's Foundation.

Primack, B.A., Shensa, A., Sidani, J.E., Whaite, E.O., Lin, L.Y., Rosen, D., Colditz, J.B., Radovic, A. and Miller, E. (2017) 'Social media use and perceived social isolation among young adults in the US', *American Journal of Preventive Medicine*, 53(1): 1–8.

Puras, D. (2017) 'Report of the Special Rapporteur on the right of everyone to the enjoyment of the highest attainable standard of physical and mental health', Human Rights Council Thirty-fifth session 6-23 June 2017 Agenda item 3. Available at: https://www.ohchr.org/EN/NewsEvents/Pages/DisplayNews.aspx?NewsID=21689

Putnam, R (2000) *Bowling Alone: The collapse and revival of American community*. New York: Simon & Schuster.

Repper, J. and Perkins, R. (2009) *Social Inclusion and Recovery*. Leiden: Elsevier.

Sin, J., Moone, N. and Harris, P. (2008) 'Siblings of individuals with first-episode psychosis: understanding their experiences and needs', *Journal of Psychosocial Nursing and Mental Health Services*, 46(6): 33–40.

Valkenburg, P. and Peter, J. (2009) 'Social consequences of the internet for adolescents: A decade of research', *Current Directions in Psychological Science*, 18(1): 1–5.

Vosoughi, S., Roy, D. and Aral, S. (2018) 'The spread of true and false news online', *Science*, 359(6380): 1146–51.

Webber, M., Morris, D., Howarth, S., Fendt-Newlin, M., Treacy, S. and McCrone, P. (2018) 'Effect of the Connecting People Intervention on social capital: a pilot study', *Research in Social Work Practice*, 29(5): 483–94.

Wolfradt, U. and Doll, J. (2001) 'Motives of adolescents to use the internet as a function of personality traits, personal and social factors', *Journal of Educational Computing Research*, 24(1): 13–27.

Yao, M. Z., and Zhong, Z. J. (2014) 'Loneliness, social contacts and Internet addiction: A cross-lagged panel study', *Computers in Human Behavior*, 30: 164–70.

6

Social media and youth justice: challenges and possibilities for practice

Naomi Thompson and Ian Joseph

Introduction

This chapter begins by exposing the lack of literature that exists relating to youth justice and social media. Current debates about young people, crime and social media are explored and critiqued. Following this, examples of social media in practice are presented. The first provides an example of young people using social media to evade the police and community orders within their local areas, demonstrating the importance of practitioners understanding and keeping pace with how young people use social media. The chapter then explores how social media has been used to enhance youth justice practice. These examples are used to analyse and explore the key issues around young people and social media for youth justice, as well as to develop some concrete recommendations for practitioners for using social media.

Young people's use of online spaces and how these link to antisocial, or even criminal, behaviour is currently a key issue of debate. Media hype and 'moral panics' around this currently focus on issues such as cyberbullying, sexting and the exploitation and grooming of young people into radicalised or abusive situations. The suicide of Hannah Smith in 2013 and the links to cyberbullying sparked a media furore (although the 2014 inquest later found she had sent abusive online messages to herself) (see, for example: BBC, 2013; Davies, 2014). The media has also actively engaged in current debates on sexting among young people, reporting on both calls for schools to report perpetrators to police (in particular, where images of young women are shared without consent) and the calls to be wary of criminalising young people around this issue (see, for example: Sawer, 2016).

A dominant media discourse about young people and social media is one of them as vulnerable to exploitation by criminals. The role of social media in the grooming of young people into Islamist radicalisation has received significant media attention, with its use to make contact with, engage and prepare the three young women from Bethnal Green to leave for Syria in 2015 being one of the most high-profile examples of this (see, for example: Khan, 2015). Similarly, the grooming of young people as victims of sexual exploitation has also been a recent media focus (see, for example: Sawer, 2016).

Recent policy has also begun to consider the role of social media and online spaces in issues relating to crime and antisocial behaviour. The Counter Extremism Strategy (Home Office, 2015) has a significant section on social media and its role in the grooming of vulnerable people, particularly the young, into radicalisation of different forms. The Serious and Organised Crime Strategy (Home Office, 2013) considers cybercrime in detail, as part of the developing forms of organised crime, though not specifically in relation to young people. Policies relating directly to youth justice, however, have yet to explicitly consider social media either as a vehicle for youth crime or in the responses to it.

There is a significant absence of research into youth justice and social media, meaning that little understanding has been sought and gained in responding to moral panics about the role of social media in crime and antisocial behaviour among young people. The related research that does exist tends to focus on the same specific and limited issues as the media and primarily on young people's vulnerability online.

Examples of this research include Ditch the Label's (2013) large-scale study into cyberbullying, which found that 7 out of 10 young people in the UK have experienced this. Research commissioned by the NSPCC into sexting and young people has found that there are clear links between sexting and cyberbullying and that threatening behaviour online is more likely to come from peers than strangers (Ringrose et al, 2012; Phippen, 2012). However, there is also an ongoing concern with the exploitation of young people online by strangers in research relating to child sexual exploitation (CEOP, 2013) while the notion of 'online radicalisation' requires further academic scrutiny (Neumann, 2013). Within the research that exists that relates to young people, crime and social media, the focus tends to be primarily on young people as potential victims rather than as perpetrators, although in some of the work explored above they are considered as both.

There is a lack of research and understanding as to how social media might impact upon and be used in youth justice practice beyond these limited issues. In particular, there has been a lack of exploration into how young people's use of social media impacts on their offline lives, routines and behaviours. Perhaps the only example of academic commentary on this in the UK is in the aftermath of the riots of summer 2011. In the LSE's (2012) investigation into the riots, they found that, although the use of Facebook and Twitter for inciting the riots had been overstated by the media during the events, the free Blackberry messaging service BBM had been used much more substantially to organise people and share information:

> This extraordinarily efficient – and secure – communications network was a key tool for many who took part in England's riots, as an easy way to share information on where looters were, safe routes home, and what police were doing. (LSE, 2012: 31)

While there were public calls to shut down the social networking sites Facebook and Twitter during the riots, the researchers' analysis of Twitter activity found that incitements to riot were largely responded to with criticism and reported to police. The site was used much more significantly in organising the clean-up operations with such tweets having a far greater reach than those relating to incitement (LSE, 2012). Academic research into how people's offline behaviour is influenced by online activity is extremely scarce across subjects, disciplines and continents, not just in UK youth justice. One of the only examples of such is the large-scale research in the US by Bond et al (2012) which found that people's offline voting behaviours in the 2010 US elections were influenced by posts made by close friends on Facebook. However, these rare examples do suggest that people's behaviour can be influenced either positively or negatively by their interactions on social media.

Another key gap in the research is any consideration of how young people's use of social media could be harnessed as a tool within practice relating to youth justice. There are ethical issues to consider in using social media as a tool in work with young people and particularly in an arena such as youth justice. In particular, the use of social media as a means of surveillance of young people is questionable. Young people are often unaware of how their public social media profiles may allow others to see into their personal lives and this has led to negative consequences for some. For example, when Kent's Police Crime Commissioner employed a Youth Crime Commissioner in 2013, she made a point of employing a young person not from a privileged background into this role as she felt this young woman would relate well to other young people. However, the media uncovered previous tweets from the young woman's public Twitter profile, exposing that she had made claims about sexual activity and drug use online among other potentially offensive topics (see, for example: Kisiel, 2013). The young woman subsequently had to step down from her role as Youth Crime Commissioner, demonstrating how, in the age of social media, young people's personal lives are subject to a level of scrutiny that those of previous generations were not. In the past, young people's 'showing off' among friends was more easily forgotten than it is today where their social media presence often means they are under the 'public gaze'. This young woman's early misdemeanours, or perhaps her exaggerated claims of such, were used to 'catch her out' in this instance and, following the media reporting of the story, are likely to haunt her for years to come.

It is clear that practitioners aiming to support young people should not be attempting to 'catch them out' in the way the media did to this young woman. However, whether and to what extent they might use social media as a means of surveillance has yet to be debated in any depth. Conradie (2015) found, in research with youth workers, that there were considerable ethical dilemmas in how practitioners might share their own personal information or access that of young people through social media. Creating work profiles to 'friend' or 'follow' young people means there is an imbalance of power in what is shared and there is a clear argument against practitioners using their personal profiles to engage with young people online. Conradie also found that some practitioners were using social media to search for personal information about young people, justifying it through the notion that anything young people shared publicly on their profiles is information that is in the 'public domain'. However, young people may not be fully aware of how they are sharing such information and who with; there is a clear ethical question about whether informed consent has been given in this context. Cheal (2014) has argued that, in line with their right to privacy within the United Nations Convention on the Rights of the Child, young people have a right to privacy and dignity in online as well as offline spaces. This means them being equipped to understand and consent to who their information is shared with. It is arguable then that practitioners working with young people have a responsibility both to educate them as to how they are sharing information online and to empower them to control who sees into their personal lives. It is ethically questionable for practitioners working with young people to intrude into young people's online spaces without their knowledge or consent. Because of the ethical questions raised by the use of social media for surveillance, this chapter will focus on developing recommendations for the positive use of social media in youth justice practice as a means of engagement. It does not advocate for the use of social media as punitive tool.

Darke (2011) argues that a 'prevent as enforcement' approach has been over-used in UK youth justice and is ineffective.

Similarly, Hughes (2011) critiques the 'law and order' discourse in the UK that focuses on the crime and not the vulnerabilities of the perpetrator. Hughes compares the response to youth crime and antisocial behaviour in England with that in Victoria, Australia – where the needs of the young person rather than the crime and its punishment are the focus of interventions – arguing that this is more effective. Similarly, Case and Haines (2015) advocate for a 'children first, offenders second' approach that treats young offenders, first and foremost, as children rather than as 'mini adults' with the same level of responsibility as actual adults. They suggest a more positive approach to youth justice is needed; their model has been tested in Swansea for a number of years and is now being implemented in other parts of the UK.

While media hype often focuses on the negatives of young people's engagement in online social spaces, virtual communication has long been recognised as a tool for building community (Rheingold, 1993). It has been acknowledged for two decades that the digital communication that takes place within cyberspace is neither more nor less real than other forms of social interaction, with the capacity existing to construct, maintain and mediate virtual communities through electronic networks (Jones, 1994). Moreover, recent technological advances have played a role in accelerating social change (Rosa, 2013). This increased pace of change has implications for the speed at which concerns about community safety shift and for the ability of policing to appropriately respond. Digital technology is seen as having huge potential for changing the relationship between government and citizen through empowering communities and encouraging civic participation (Loveridge, 2014). Rapid changes in information and communication technology are creating new opportunities for cybercrime and, as such, are also having profound effects on modern-day policing not only in the UK but in developments across Europe (Denef, 2011).

There is, however, a lack of research into how young people use social media in positive and negative ways. As such, there is much catching up to do by both researchers and practitioners in regards to understanding young people's use of social media to interact, communicate and belong, particularly in relation to youth justice. Conradie (2015), in research with youth workers, found that there is a lack of practice guidance on using social media in work with young people and that neither policy nor practice have kept pace with advances in online technologies. She found that a lack of policies and specific guidelines within youth services has led both to some practitioners avoiding using it where it might enhance their work and others engaging in questionable forms of practice through social media. While she found that many managers were generally in support of their staff finding ways of harnessing social media, they were also unclear as to how to guide them in doing so. Key issues included what information practitioners should be able to access about the young people they work with through social media profiles and vice versa. What is clear is that there is much work to be done in exploring how social media might be used in work with young people more generally and in relation to youth justice. This chapter aims to explore and develop some recommendations for the latter.

Geographical versus online space and community

The following case example shows the potential tension between social work based on spaces defined on traditional geographic definitions and young people's capacity to redefine their own spaces using social media.

Example: Evading authority

A few years ago, one of this chapter's authors worked as a street-based youth worker in a small city in the north of England. The city is surrounded by small suburban villages in close proximity to each other, a short distance from the city and all within or just outside its ring road with good bus connections. The youth worker worked for a ward that included a few of these closely populated villages. While youth crime in the area was actually relatively low, community perception of it was high within the ward.

Because of the prevalence of complaints from local residents about groups of young people 'hanging around', a number of police measures were used in an attempt to prevent young people gathering in groups of a size perceived as threatening by others. Groups of young people were regularly 'stopped and searched', with anti-terror legislation allowing police to search people without evidence of wrongdoing. Temporary police orders were implemented in quick succession; these included curfew orders, where young people had to be off the streets in the evenings, and dispersal orders, where no groups of two or more young people were permitted to gather together in the evenings in public spaces.

For street-based youth workers employed by the local authority, these measures were at odds with our work engaging young people on the streets. Young people began to gather in more hidden spaces that were not only more difficult to find, they were less likely to be safe and more likely to involve trespassing onto private land. Indeed, young people told us that the very reason they had chosen to gather in the more central community spaces, where they were perceived as a nuisance, such as outside the village shops, near main bus stops or community buildings, was because these places were well lit.

Young people were criminalised by these orders, not just because previously legitimate behaviour became forbidden, but because they were pushed to gather in illegal spaces. Essentially, such orders only served to reinforce a sense of exclusion among local young people, sending a message to them they were not part of their communities, that they were problematic outsiders and cementing a feeling of hostility and of 'them and us' between young people and the police as well as their wider communities. While the intention of the orders was that young people would not gather at all, the young people told us that it also felt like *their* safety was not a priority. When they were found by the police on patrol in the area in groups of more than two during the dispersal order, for example, the police would order them to split off into ones and pairs and would wait while they all walked away in different directions. (Some of the youngest were taken home by police.)

From our ongoing engagement with the young people, we observed that the police orders only motivated the young people to create their own spaces for community and belonging together as the excluded group. Modern technology meant that these spaces could be online as well as physical spaces, and online social networking also offered the opportunity for them to organise themselves and communicate with each other about where the physical spaces might be.

Example: Evading authority (continued)

In one of the communities that was perhaps most aggressively targeted by the curfew and dispersal orders, we continued for a while to find the local young people in new, less open spaces, such as between blocks of garages or in the dark space behind the village shops. The young people told us about how the police began to find them in these places and move them on, after further complaints were made. Eventually, one particular evening we did not find any young people at all in this community, despite having been working with them at the same regular time over a substantial period.

The next evening, we were working in one of the villages outside the ring road and encountered a larger than usual group of young people outside the local shops. This group contained young people not just from that particular village but also from the one we had visited the evening before, as well as others we did not know. The young people explained that they were using an online messaging service to liaise with their friends from the two local high schools about where police were targeting and which areas were 'safe' to gather. Over time, the groups we encountered became larger and the young people increasingly came from further afield, including from the villages and suburbs on the other side of the city. Some evenings we did not see young people at all. Others, we encountered up to 50 at a time in one space. In the village just outside of the ring road, where we had first encountered this migration of groups, the local Co-op invested in a mosquito alarm (a high-pitched alarm that only people below a certain age can hear). The use of these alarms, although through private rather than public investment, arguably only reinforced the sense of exclusion felt by the young people. It is notable that such alarms, in their original forms, were developed to emit frequencies that no humans could hear and were used to deter mice from people's houses or cats from gardens. (Whether the use of a technology developed to scare away animals is appropriate as a tool of age discrimination is a whole debate in itself and there is not space to develop it here.) The young people moved to another village in our area before disappearing altogether for a while, later explaining they had been meeting in a village outside of the boundaries of the area we worked in.

This process of migrating to different areas was only facilitated by the use on online messaging. Through this, young people were able to not only create and gather in an 'online space', but to organise themselves to meet in physical spaces that transcended the geographical boundaries of the local authority youth workers for that particular ward, as well as move between areas of different police responsibility.

This case example demonstrates the futility of the geographically bound police orders imposed on the young people, not simply because they only served to reinforce a sense of exclusion among young people, but because advances in social media allowed the young people to evade these orders by moving between physical boundaries. The online space arguably also served as an 'un-intruded' place for them to gather and communicate in virtual form. It also reinforces how practitioners, in this case both police and youth workers (but the argument extends to all those working with young people), need to keep pace with young people's use of social media. They need not just to understand how young people are using social media but to adapt their work accordingly. In this case, working within the geographical boundaries of a particular area hampered both the police and the youth workers' practice. The young people's use of online messaging demonstrates their ability to use social media to create their own community, organise themselves and communicate in a social space within which they define who is included or not.

For an age group increasingly excluded from their geographical communities through being seen as problematic or even criminalised, it is unsurprising that online spaces have become more significant in young people's lives. The young people in this case study were, in one sense, building a virtual community, as discussed earlier (Rheingold, 1993; Jones, 1994). However, they were also, and perhaps more significantly, using social media to organise offline activity. Their use of online messaging has clear links to the LSE's (2012) findings about the use of messaging during the riots in 2011. Just as the US research mentioned earlier found that people's offline voting behaviours in presidential elections were influenced by posts made by close friends on social media (Bond et al, 2012), it is arguable that the young people in this context may also be using social media as a space for influencing the offline 'political', community and protest activity of their friends.

Using social media positively in practice

The chapters in this book provide several examples of positive use of social media. In particular the next chapter (Chapter 7) offers a good example of how to develop an online community and demonstrates how online communities can be used to support practice and practitioners, and to promote better understanding of the profession and its values. In what follows, the authors highlight another example of positive use of social media for consultation with young people around youth involvement in gang activity and serious violence. This example of the positive use of social media emerged from responses to the killing of a thirteen-year-old boy in a deprived area of London. This took place at a time of a growing voluntary, community and social enterprise sector consensus about shortfalls in the ability of mainstream services to both adequately understand how and why young people become involved in serious youth violence as well as to keep pace with the tools and technologies which might be used in the response.

Example: Tackling violence through #OneBigDebate

The killing of a thirteen-year-old boy inspired a close friend to work with his community and local organisations to foster community action aimed at tackling youth violence at the local level. The 'One Big Community' (OBC) was thus set up in 2013 as a London-wide youth-led coalition committed to ending youth violence by engaging young people directly in decision-making processes and empowering them to make real bottom-up change. Quickly progressing into a youth-led coalition of 40 organisations, with a 25 strong youth management committee, it set out to devise and deliver a consultation programme that would provide youth perspectives as counternarratives to 'taken for granted' understandings of gangs and young people. This consultation enabled the direct involvement of over 4,500 young people in a critical debate on how far current policy and practice effectively tackles youth violence, using up-to-date online technologies as one of its tools, and attracted regional press coverage. One of the consultation events was 'One Big Debate', an online opportunity for young people to share their views and experiences of gangs and violence. The event explored issues raised directly by young people, using key questions to guide a live online debate on social media and via a survey. This was the first stage of a more extensive youth consultation.

Although the press and other traditional methods were also used, online technologies were the primary means of advertising the event, disseminating the date, time, location and how to sign up the debate via email blasts and via social media. The event started with 150 on-site participants gathering in the main hall of a south London school before being split into groups and taken into classrooms around the school where they had access to computers for the online debate. The debate was structured around tweeted responses to ten questions that had been developed by the OBC management committee and were introduced at appropriate junctures over a six-hour period. During this exchange of views and opinions, young people at the venue were joined by others from all over the country, and even some from outside of the UK. The discussion attracted over 3,600 tweets, reaching a calculated 20,000 people and trended top of the UK Twitter rankings with the hashtag #OneBigDebate.

After the event, under the supervision of the OBC management committee, a group of volunteers analysed the results of the survey and Twitter responses (see Table 6.1).

Analysis of the tweets from during the event showed an overwhelmingly positive online response to the overall debate.

Questions attracting the largest number of responses and strongest views focused on two issues in particular. A long series of retweets demonstrated that although many young people encountered violence in their everyday routines, the media were seen as propagating a culture of fear. One person summarising the exchange of opinion about the role of the press tweeted:

> **#OneBigDebate** Media must stop treating youth like Aeroplanes. [They] Only report on ones that crash

Crucially, the overwhelming view was that many did not see 'gangs' as a major cause of experienced violence, with only 6% directly attributing it to gang activity. Debates on this topic prompted the largest number of retweets, with many reflecting the following view:

> **#OneBigDebate** gang is too vague a term. The word gang could refer to multiple things, we need to be more precise with terms and definitions

Table 6.1: Results of the One Big Debate Survey

	Yes (%)	No (%)	Don't know (%)
1. Do you know any young people who have died/been seriously injured as a result of youth violence?	69	31	0
2. Do you believe there is a solution to youth violence?	62	19	19
3. Do rivalries that lead to youth violence start at school?	58	25	17
4. Do you trust the police?	20	57	23
5. Do you believe the police can keep you safe?	25	60	15
6. Do you think there would be less youth violence if there were more job opportunities for young people?	87	5	8
7. Is all youth violence associated with gangs?	6	94	0
8. Is enough attention paid to female victims of youth violence?	10	60	30
9. Is the media a contributing factor to youth violence?	72	9	19
10. Would you like to be actively involved in decisions about community safety?	84	8	8

Overall, the One Big Debate event allowed for the positive use of social media to engage young people and practitioners in discussion about some key youth justice issues. There are some key positive recommendations that can be drawn from this case example for the use of social media in practice. Most pertinently, it challenges the dominant negativity about young people's use of social media by using it to build community and foster critical debate. In this case example, social media is used in both a positive and ethical way to engage with young people, as opposed to a means of surveillance.

Developing youth justice practice around social media

Social media is a huge part of young people's lives and this is unlikely to change. Young people need to understand the impact their engagement with social media might have on their lives and practitioners need to understand how young people use it and for what ends, as well as how online activity links to offline behaviour. Young people seek both private spaces (through messaging services, for example) and public engagement (through public posts on social media) in their online communications. Practitioners need to understand and, indeed, respect the nuances in young people's online activity and develop clear protocols for how, where and when it is appropriate to engage with young people in their online worlds. There is clear potential for practitioners' engagement with young people in understanding and sensitively using social media. Positive online campaigns can be, and indeed, have been, used to combat negative perceptions of young people. One example is the #notinmyname campaign, sparked after the 2011 riots by NCVYS (the National Council for Voluntary Youth Services) for young people to make their stand against the riots and to demonstrate that many young people did not support them. Practitioners can, as such, use social media to encourage collective debate and online community rather than avoiding it, invading it (as a means of surveillance) or seeking to shut it down.

Young people are already using online communications to organise themselves and coordinate action. In the first case example on evading authority, young people's use of social media messaging services to organise themselves is strikingly similar to how it was used in the 2011 riots (LSE, 2012). The use of Twitter for more positive activism in the One Big Debate (see the second case example) makes a strong case for how social media can be channelled for constructive debate with young people, rather than viewed as an entirely negative phenomenon. Again, the finding that social media, particularly Twitter, was used more substantively to organise the clean-up operations rather than the riots themselves in 2011 highlights the potential of social media activism for positive action (LSE, 2012).

The biggest issue that prevents youth practitioners from using social media is the lack of clear guidelines available for how to do this (Conradie, 2015). Before social media can be used by youth justice practitioners on a large scale, the appropriate policies and procedures need to be developed and these are currently scarce, if not completely non-existent. Alongside this, more research is needed as to how practitioners can use social media to enhance their work with young people and to inform such policies. The protocols developed need to be reflexive and able to evolve as technology advances and the sites that young people use change. There should be some clear underlying principles that relate to young people's privacy and rights as well as the professional boundaries of practitioners – alongside specific guidelines for different sites.

Alongside clear guidelines for practice, training needs to be developed and provided to youth justice practitioners – again, this needs to be flexible, responsive and informed by research – but with clear overall principles around rights, privacies and professional conduct online. In particular, youth justice practitioners need to understand not just how young people may engage in or encounter problematic behaviours online but also how online activity informs offline behaviours. They need to be able to work with young people's use of social media and not simply against it, fostering online dialogue for positive change, debate and action as in the One Big Debate example in this chapter or the example of the community of practice in the next chapter. They also need to be aware of the fluidity of borders online – where geographical boundaries no longer exist. As seen in the first example in this chapter, young people are migrating between and moving beyond different geographical areas facilitated by their online communications. This has implications for practitioners such as youth workers, police and other professionals who have a specific geographical remit. Collaboration and communication across geographical areas will be crucial in keeping pace with young people's use of social media to organise themselves, rather than simply removing 'problems' from one authority area into another. Young people have demonstrated, both in the practice example given here and through their online communications during the 2011 riots, that social media allows them to navigate between and across geographical boundaries according to where is being targeted punitively or where they are currently undisturbed. This sophisticated use of social media to communicate quickly and effectively about where to gather is too efficient for area-bound orders and practitioners to keep pace with.

Any policies and training developed around the use of social media in practice need to consider the ethics of online engagement. As mentioned, young people's rights, particularly in relation to privacy, need to be maintained. Practitioners need to consider what is appropriate in terms of online interactions. For example, it would not be appropriate for professionals to use their personal social media accounts to engage with young people and they also need to recognise the power dynamic that exists if they use professional accounts to connect with young people's personal profiles which give access to their personal lives. It is arguable that professional 'best practice' would be to not become 'friends' or 'followers' of young people's social media profiles but to create pages or groups that the young people can choose to connect with and to what extent to engage with. Such a strategy makes it less easy for practitioners' social media contact with young people to involve surveillance of young people – or at least limits what practitioners can view only to what the young person has made 'public'. While youth justice does involve some level of surveillance or monitoring of young people, this should be treated with the same respect for public and private space as offline surveillance would be, with anything shared only with 'friends' or 'followers' treated as private space online. This would fit with the ethical 'good practice' suggested by Baker (2013) for research with young people online – as well as best practice guidance provided by Buzzi and Megele (2020) which draws on the PSW national research and practice development project led by the editors of this book. Practitioners should arguably maintain similar ethical boundaries. It should also be recognised that young people are not always aware of what can be viewed publicly on their social media profiles, and therefore their consent for others to view anything 'public' cannot be assumed (Baker, 2013; Buzzi and Megele, 2020). It would be ethical, therefore, to ensure that it is made explicit to young people what the purposes are of engaging with them via social media, and how their data will be used, as would be done for any data they share offline. The implications of the Data Protection Act (1998) and the General Data Protection Regulation (GDPR) as well as safeguarding legislation should be considered for online engagement in the same way they are in offline engagement, with young people made fully aware of their rights to confidentiality as well as the legal limitations to this.

As outlined in the discussions in this chapter already, it is not engagement with social media as a form of surveillance of young people that we advocate for – but for using social media as a positive rather than a punitive tool for practice. Young people also need to be educated and made aware of the limitations to their privacy on social media and of their rights to control what is available to whom. They need to be supported in learning how to use social media constructively and how to deal with negative encounters online. They need to protect themselves on several levels including from abuse in order to combat bullying, to preserve their mental health from the anxieties that can be caused by online encounters and visibility, and to prevent the most extreme tragedies such as suicide. They also need to be aware of what is appropriate behaviour online, to avoid being the perpetrator of antisocial or even criminal online behaviour – and to avoid unwittingly incriminating themselves with what they share online, as in the case of Kent's Youth Crime Commissioner discussed earlier.

Conclusion

Social media poses some clear challenges and opportunities for youth justice. Young people's online engagement needs to be understood as to its impact on offline behaviours as well as in terms of what behaviour is problematic in the online spaces themselves. Young people and practitioners need to understand the boundaries between public and private space online and young people should be made clearly aware of how any data they share with practitioners online will be used. This chapter has argued for a positive rather than a punitive use of social media, resisting the 'law and order' and 'prevent as enforcement' discourses which have been found to be less effective than positive engagement in youth justice practice (Darke, 2011; Hughes, 2011).

As such, the key practical implications developed in this chapter are around the possibilities of social media to work collaboratively with young people. There is also a need for education for young people in using social media positively, highlighting issues around privacy, incrimination and cyberbullying among others so they are fully aware. Organisations such as CEOP have made some clear ground on this but recent media examples of the problematic use of social media by young people suggest there is still some way to go.

There is a need for clear guidelines, bespoke training and more research into engaging with young people online as youth justice professionals. The recent best practice guidance by the PSW national research and practice development project provide a clear and much needed ethical framework for practitioners and their employers. Such guidelines are essential and without them practice cannot be developed in a consistent, ethical and explicit form. Individual organisations need to begin to develop clear procedures as well as clear aims as to the purposes of engagement with young people online that are explicit to young people as well as practitioners.

From an ethical perspective, the use of social media as a form of surveillance into young people's private lives is questionable. A simplistic analysis of the first practice example given in this chapter could lead to a recommendation for more surveillance of and intrusion into young people's online spaces. This is not what this chapter argues for. The second example demonstrates how social media can be used in a positive way with young people and it is this that this chapter advocates for. The first highlights a need to keep pace with how young people use social media. This knowledge can be used to develop positive interventions with young people that draw on their chosen methods of communication, rather than used as justification for 'spying' on them in their peer group spaces.

Young people will continue to seek out spaces to build community and interact with their peers. Indeed, the first example demonstrates that the more we insist on intruding into these spaces in a punitive fashion the more they will seek new spaces. Therefore, the key recommendations of this chapter are that young people's right to belong and create community space online be respected but that these spaces can be used appropriately by sensitive practitioners who wish to engage with them there in positive and collaborative ways.

References

Baker, S. (2013) 'Conceptualising the use of Facebook in ethnographic research: as tool, as data and as context', *Ethnography and Education*, 8(2): 131–45.

BBC (2013) 'Hannah Smith death: father says daughter was victim of cyberbullies' (6 August 2013). Available at: http://www.bbc.co.uk/news/uk-england-leicestershire-23584769

Bond, R. M., Fariss, C. J., Jones, J. J., Kramer, A. D. I., Marlow, C., Settle, J. E. and Fowler, J. H. (2012) 'A 61-million-person experiment in social influence and political mobilization', *Nature*, 489(7415): 295–8.

Buzzi, P. and Megele, C. (2020) *Digital Practice and Working with Children and Young People Online*. London: PSW Network.

Case, S. and Haines, K. (2015) *Positive Youth Justice*, Bristol: Policy Press.

CEOP (2013) *Threat Assessment of Child Sexual Exploitation and Abuse (June 2013)*. London: Child Exploitation and Online Protection Centre.

Cheal, S. (2014) 'The rights of a child relating to content shared about them through social media, with a particular focus on Facebook'. Unpublished MA thesis, London: YMCA George Williams College.

Colander, D. and Kupers, R. (2014) *Complexity and the Art of Public Policy: Solving society's problems from the bottom up*. New Jersey: Princeton University Press.

Conradie, L. (2015) 'Rethinking personal and professional boundaries between young people and youth work practitioners as manifested through connections on online social network sites', *yresearch*, 1: 57–70.

Darke, S. (2011) 'The enforcement approach to crime prevention', *Critical Social Policy*, 31(3): 410–30.

Davies, C. (2014) 'Hannah Smith wrote "vile" posts to herself before suicide, say police', *The Guardian* (6 May 2014). Available at: http://www.theguardian.com/uk-news/2014/may/06/hannah-smith-suicide-teenager-cyber-bullying-inquests

Denef, S, (2011) 'ICT Trends in European Policing. COMPOSITE Draft of Deliverables D4.1'. Available at: https://www.fit.fraunhofer.de/content/dam/fit/de/documents/composite_d41.pdf.

Ditch the Label (2013) 'The Annual Cyber-bullying Survey 2013'. Available at: http://www.ditchthelabel.org/the-cyber-bullying-survey-2013/.

Foth, M. (2006) 'Network action research', *Action Research*, 4(2): 205–26.

Hallsworth, S. (2014) 'Gang talking criminologists: A rejoinder to John Pitts', *Youth and Policy*, 112: 35–43.

Home Office (2013) 'Serious and Organised Crime Strategy', London: Home Office.

Home Office (2015) *Counter Extremism Strategy*. London: Home Office.

Hughes, N. (2011) 'Young people "as risk" or young people "at risk": Comparing discourses of anti-social behaviour in England and Victoria', *Critical Social Policy*, 31(3): 388–409.

ITV (2014) 'ITV London visits One Big Community's Wall of Silence event'. Available at: https://www.youtube.com/watch?v=1ALuVlKV0yk&feature=youtu.be

Khan, S. (2015) 'The jihadi girls who went to Syria weren't just radicalised by ISIS – they were groomed', *The Independent* (25 February 2015). Available at: http://www.independent.co.uk/voices/comment/the-jihadi-girls-who-went-to-syria-werent-just-radicalised-by-isis-they-were-groomed-10069109.html

Kisiel, R. (2013) 'Foul-mouthed teen crime tsar QUITS her £15,000-a-year youth commissioner role after police launch investigation into Twitter rant', Mailonline (9 April 2013). Available at: http://www.dailymail.co.uk/news/article-2306335/Paris-Brown-QUITS-15-000-year-youth-commissioner-role-police-launch-investigation-Twitter-rant.html

Loveridge, L. (2014) *Communities That Work: Empowering communities and encouraging civic participation through innovative digital applications*. London: Winston Churchill Memorial Trust.

LSE (2012) *Reading the Riots*. London: London School of Economics. Available at: http://eprints.lse.ac.uk/46297/1/Reading%20the%20riots(published).pdf

Neumann, P. R. (2013) 'The trouble with radicalization', *International Affairs*, 89(4): 873–93.

Phippen, A. (2012) *Sexting: An exploration of practices, attitudes and influences*, London: NSPCC. Available at: https://www.nspcc.org.uk/globalassets/documents/research-reports/sexting-exploration-practices-attitudes-influences-report-2012.pdf

Rheingold, H. (1993) *The Virtual Community: Homesteading on the electronic frontier*. Reading, MA: Addison-Wesley.

Ringrose, J., Gill, R., Livingstone, S. and Harvey, L. (2012) *A Qualitative Study of Children, Young People and 'Sexting'*. London: NSPCC. Available at: https://www.nspcc.org.uk/globalassets/documents/research-reports/qualitative-study-children-young-people-sexting-report.pdf

Rosa, H. (2013) *Social Acceleration: A new theory of modernity*. Columbia: Columbia University Press.

Sawer, P. (2016) 'Wave of sexting by school children raises fears of grooming', *The Telegraph* (12 March). Available at: http://www.telegraph.co.uk/education/educationnews/12191946/Wave-of-sexting-by-school-children-raises-fears-of-grooming.html

7

Social media and 'communities of practice' and 'communities of interest'

Claudia Megele and Peter Buzzi

Introduction

This chapter examines the dimensions and dynamics of online 'communities of practice' (CoP) and 'communities of interest' (CoP) and their characteristics and relevance to social work and social care practice and education. After a brief introduction highlighting the changes in mobility and technology and their impact and the emergence of online communities, to ground the discussion in practice, the chapter presents as an example the first social work 'Twitter chat' and community of practice. Reflecting on the formation and development of @SWSCmedia community, the first author (Claudia Megele) draws some of the learnings from that experience to distinguish between online networks and communities and to examine the dynamics and use of communities of practice as a source of learning and knowledge generation as well as professional formation and identity development for both individuals and professions. Thinking about communities of practice as a multilogue conversation, the authors examine the impact and ramifications of communities of practice for professional identity and considers some of the challenges and opportunities associated with communities of practice and communities of interest. The chapter concludes with some reflections and general considerations in relation to creation, development and coordination of communities of practice and interest.

The 'traditional' concept of community was based on spatial proximity (that is physical closeness, such as a neighbourhood) and a common cause or obligation or values, combined with trust, reciprocity, and a sense of belonging. However, the 'traditional' concept and dynamics of community have been greatly impacted and substantially transformed by increased mobility among populations, aided more recently by mobile technologies. Indeed, as modern technologies offered increased mobility they also introduced many distances into everyday living, impacting and supplanting the spatial proximity of communities and threatening their very survival. In the same manner, the ease and increase in overall mobility impacted individuals' social networks, including family and close relationships. Today, families and friends are often scattered around the globe, and home and work may be in different localities, cities, or even countries. Such distances, combined with the increasing pace and demands of everyday living, make it difficult for face-to-face communities to be the predominant social 'reality' in contemporary society (Gergen, 1991).

However, the emergence of new communication technologies – from telegraph and telephone to internet and social media and digital technologies – transcends geographic boundaries and allows people to connect, communicate, exchange ideas and information, build and maintain relationships and develop and enhance their social network across the globe. These changes offer new possibilities for remaining in touch and a new notion of proximity, superseding the need for spatial closeness as a prerequisite for creation of communities. Furthermore, with 24-hour connectivity, connectedness is the 'default mode' for contemporary society and for individual identities (that is, it is perceived to be the norm and often taken for granted).

As the communicative and sharing capabilities of new media are increasingly embedded in new and emerging technologies they add a 'social' dimension, transforming these into social technologies (Megele with Buzzi, 2017). These transformations have important implications for human sociality, relationships, identity, empathy and the creation of communities.

Due to the synchronous and asynchronous capabilities of digital and social media technologies, online/virtual communities of practice and communities of interest offer new possibilities for rich and dynamic conversations that can generate a sense of belonging, enhance personal and professional identities, and create significant new and imaginative opportunities and potential.

Indeed, communities of practice and communities of interest are more than a space for exchange of information, they facilitate a meeting of minds and ideas and allow for a continuous cycle of reflective learning and development; in this sense, communities of practice can be thought of as continuous learning conversations (Megele, 2014a; Megele with Buzzi, 2017).

The emergence of online communities of practice

In exploring communities of practice and their development and impact and to ground the discussion in practice, this chapter draws on the experience (see case example box) of the formation, development and facilitation of the first social work Twitter chat and community of practice (@SWSCmedia). We will use this example to explore and demonstrate the transformation of the digital and social media landscape and the strengths, opportunities and challenges associated with communities of practice and interest.

Most of the mainstream media attention directed towards social workers tends to be negative (Jones, 2012), with social work and social workers either ignored or pilloried in traditional media for 'mistakes made and lessons not learnt'. In the absence of a publicly and positively recognised professional identity and narrative for social work, media reports about social work have traditionally offered a sensationalised and unbalanced versions of events and social work interventions, often leading to harassment of practitioners as the consequence of a sort of 'trial by media'. Therefore, in 2011 the first author created the first Social Work Twitter chat as an online community of practice to support social workers.

Example: Social Work and Media (@SWSCmedia)

In July 2011, I created the LinkedIn group 'Social Work and Media' with the objective of providing a digital space for social workers to discuss social work practice and the challenges facing the profession and to create a space for reflection that could bridge the gap between theory and practice and highlight the challenges in practice and what social work was 'really' like and its positive impact in people's lives and society.. Although the LinkedIn group was well received and rapidly gained in membership, this was a closed group and, therefore, could not openly evidence social work narratives. Given the continued sensationalisation and frequent misrepresentation of the profession, I felt there was a need for an open online community that could provide an accurate counternarrative and highlight the complexity of social work practice by acknowledging and celebrating the good work and dedication of social work practitioners. Therefore, after consulting with other practitioners, on 8 October 2011, I created a Twitter account for the 'Social Work and Media Network' (@SWSCmedia and hashtag #SWSCMedia), with the intention of conducting weekly Twitter chats as an open forum and online community that could evidence authentic social work narratives and the lived experience of social work practitioners and people who access services, highlighting the challenges, intricacies and complexities of practice.

The first social work Twitter chat was held on 18 October 2011. This was the first time for social workers to participate in an open online debate about social work on social media. Given the landscape, I was acutely aware that, in spite of its positive potential, an open discussion on social media about social work could also entail a number of possible challenges and repercussions, including inappropriate, biased or derogatory expressions, posting and behaviour by participants belonging to anti-social work groups or others. Additionally, many of my peers expressed concerns that I might be personally targeted and trolled on social media for starting an online community for social workers. However, in spite of the anxieties and concerns and the heavy burden of unpredictable online reactions, I felt that it was necessary for social work and social workers to be able to evidence their own narrative and tell their own stories.

The first chat was very well received, with a large number of participants taking part; these included social work practitioners, social work academics, researchers, various organisations as well as some journalists/ columnists from the trade press. After all the trepidation, it was a huge relief to note that there was no untoward incident. Indeed, there was a great atmosphere and a rich and diverse mix of ideas and interactions among participants. The following tweet at the end of @SWSCmedia's inaugural chat encapsulates this:

> We've seen the future! We were present at the creation. #swscmedia

---

The social media landscape has changed significantly since. However, the concerns, reticence and fear of participation that dominated the atmosphere in 2011 are encapsulated in this tweet addressed to @SWSCmedia by @BASW_UK:

> **BASW_UK** BASW

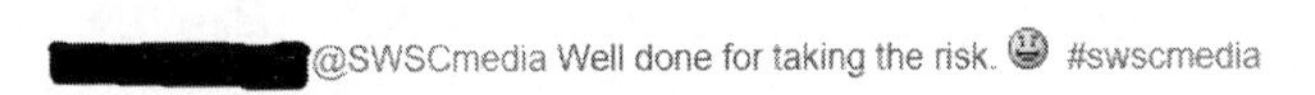

Driven by the request from social work students, in February 2012, in addition to its regular chats every Tuesday, @SWSCmedia community began weekly student chats, every Sunday, followed by additional social work chats in the US and Canada on every Wednesday. All chats were accompanied by a relevant blog; as a result the Social Work and Media blog provides a range of rich and helpful articles and discussions about the chats and other relevant topics.

A decade later, social media is now commonly used by many social workers for a variety of purposes and social work has a much better presence on social media with a multiplicity of voices and communities. Today there are various Twitter chats, Facebook groups, communities of practice and communities of interest that could be relevant for social workers. Indeed, the hashtag #SocialWork on Twitter offers a rich source of information and news about social work. The international and national associations of social workers' social media accounts (such as @BASW_UK and @NASW) offer a range of resources and information as well as online communities of practice.

Mental Health Chat (@MHChat), *The Guardian* newspaper's social care (@GdnSocialCare) networks, the 'US Social Work' podcast by Dr Jonathan Singer and the 'UK Social Work' podcast by David Niven are examples of other online communities that offer excellent, relevant and valuable resources and information on a range of important topics in social work. NSPCC, Skills for Care, Social Care Institute for Excellence, *The Guardian*'s other professional networks, *Community Care* (@CommunityCare), *New Social Worker* magazine and community, *Social Work Today* magazine and community, the PSW network for children and families/social workers and adult services are all further examples of social work resources, websites, and communities online. Indeed, on any day of the week and almost any hour of the day, practitioners can find a chat or discussion or a community of practice that may be of interest and relevant to social work. This has changed the narrative of social work.

However, in 2011, Twitter chats were a relatively new phenomenon and a first in social work. The open and inclusive nature of the @SWSCmedia community (comprised of practitioners, students, academics, researchers, people who access services, universities, service providers, policy makers, and other individuals and organisations), the immediacy of interactions and the unstructured nature of the chats broke down the traditional hierarchies, supplanting them with dynamic heterarchies and empowering relationships between participants. This was enriched with the diversity of ideas and participants as noted in *Community Care* article, 'Which debate tells us most about social work today; NCAS or Twitter?'.

To enhance the discussions and their impact, most of @SWSCmedia debates/chats followed an extended reflective cycle (see Figure 7.1).

The debate cycle and the processes of weekly chats began with a blog post to announce the topic and to provide background and context for the discussion. To encourage reflection, the blog included a number of relevant questions that were subsequently discussed during the online chat.

To further enrich the discussions, subject experts were invited as special guests. A blog by the special guest provided further food for thought and was often accompanied by more blog posts

Figure 7.1: The @SWSCmedia's reflective cycle of knowledge generation

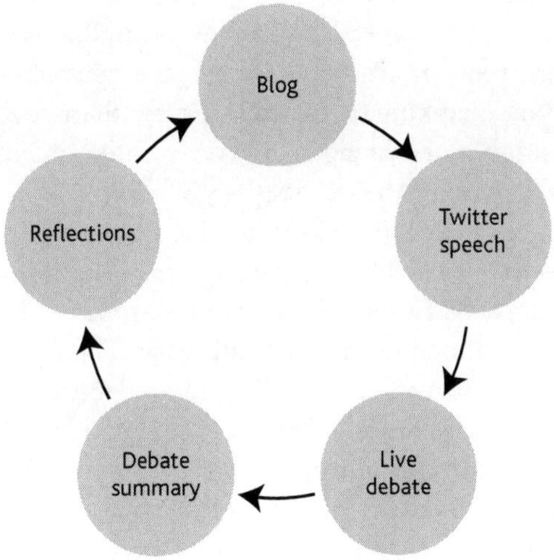

Blog
Twitter speech
Live debate
Debate summary
Reflections

Source: Adapted from Megele, 2015

from others (practitioners, users of services, academics, students, organisations, or others), adding multiple views on the topic and enriching both the substance and context of the debate.

The actual chat then began with a series of tweets (labelled as a 'Twitter speech') posted by the special guest in a sequence of rapid tweets at the beginning of the chat to provide background and context for the pursuing discussion and debate @SWSCmedia. These tweets drew the participants' attention to some of the more salient points and were followed by @SWSCmedia posting the first question from the blog and the open debate among participants. Although @SWSCmedia engaged with various participants both to acknowledge their contribution and to moderate by asking for further elaboration of their points, it should be noted that, given the unrestricted and unstructured nature of a Twitter chat, it is the community rather than any specific social media user or account that moderates the chat and the community space. Hence, often discussions developed in multiple directions and as a multilogue conversation. Various questions from the blog were then posted by @SWSCmedia on Twitter and at different intervals. The engagement from @SWSCmedia was aimed at promoting exchange of ideas and experiences, and facilitating discussion and a multiplicity of views.

The chats were closed by @SWSCmedia with a few concluding tweets briefly summarising the salient points from the debate and thanking the participants for their contributions and for joining and sharing their views. Subsequently, tweets were collected using the hashtag #SWSCmedia and the chat transcript was posted on SWSCmedia website. However, to ensure everyone's voice was preserved, rather than selecting a few representative tweets for the chat summary, all collected tweets were included in the chat summary. The chat summary served (and still serves) as a resource for reflection and further discussion and elaboration of experiences and ideas.

This process and the concepts of a 'Twitter speech' and using multiple blogs with diverse views to set the context for each debate were innovative at the time, and proved effective and powerful in generating a strong positive narrative and rich space for social work debates and discussions. Although it seemed that the debates took place rather effortlessly, the reflective knowledge generation cycle used by @SWSCmedia involved extensive preparation and background work, from deciding the topic and announcing it on SWSCmedia blog to inviting weekly guests, preparing Twitter speeches, inviting bloggers with relevant knowledge, receiving, editing, agreeing and posting their blogs, moderating comments and feedback, responding to online enquiries and engaging with participants, and so on. As is usually the case, although online chats may seem simple and easy to replicate they require preparation; in fact, the more effortless the debate may seem, often the more detailed planning and background work it requires.

These online discussions attracted participants from over 35 countries with diverse views, backgrounds, experiences, expertise and cultural perspectives. The Social Work and Media (@SWSCmedia) community became a great example of coproduction, collective leadership and leaderful practice in social work. Furthermore, the weekly schedule of the chats enabled the community to quickly react and discuss topical issues and challenges as they unfolded, ranging from government policies and consultations to new initiatives such as the launch of the Frontline Academy.

Often different social workers, social work students, or people who access services tweeted under the community account @SWSCmedia and – although a log was kept of the name, time and duration each person tweeted under the community account – this information and the identities of the people tweeting under the community account were not revealed to others. This helped ensure that the community space reflected the voices of its members and participants over and above anyone facilitating the chat or tweeting for @SWSCmedia. In this manner, the Social Work and Media (@SWSCmedia) community offered an open space for everyone's voice without being dominated by any single voice.

The 'Trending' column on the right hand side of Twitter screen lists the top 10 discussions based on number of participants and tweets at any given time, and several times, @SWSCmedia's chat hashtag #SWSCmedia trended on Twitter. It was especially gratifying to see social work trending on Twitter for positive practice rather than the negative media messages and images.

@SWSCmedia debates and discussions promoted coproduction and pioneered an innovative and powerful approach for promoting social work values and practice. It also provided a space for the meeting of minds and the validation of practitioners' experiences and served as a creative and developmental space offering opportunities for knowledge creation, ideas generation, and identity work. The chats covered a wide range of topics including frontline practice, supervision, leadership and more. The diversity of ideas expanded the breadth of idea and participants' perspectives and encouraged reflexive and reflective engagements and discussions. Such reflective and networked discussions and ideas offer a rich source for rendering tacit knowledge explicit and for the development of insight as 'recognition of patterns and structures' (Dane and Pratt, 2007, p 37) that reflect the complexities and intricacies of practice.

Aside from evidencing, upholding and witnessing lived narratives of social work and bridging theory and practice divide, the Social Work and Media (@SWSCmedia) community offered a holding space and served as a mirror for community members and participants to discover self-reflectively or bounce off their ideas and experiences and through cycle of enquiry, engagement, conversation and reflection move from confusion to comprehension (Dominowski and Dallob, 1995, p 37).

The @SWSCmedia community provided a space for unpacking the lived narratives of both the joys and challenges of social work through the retelling of practitioners' stories, thoughts and feelings and those of the people who access services. Capturing and rendering of participants' experiences and views generated important practice wisdom, while witnessing narratives of everyday social work served as a counternarrative, challenging the popular media's soundbite and instrumental reductionisms of social work and its practice.

@SWSCmedia and communities of practice/interest

Online/virtual communities are multilogue conversations

Traditional offline communications are usually unidirectional (that is, from speaker, as sender of message/information, to audience as receiver(s) of information). However, online conversations using digital or social media technologies are usually multilogue conversations, as Megele (2014a) explains:

> Multilogue is a many-to-many communication, where each message is addressed to more than one potential receiver and may be answered by more than one potential respondent. Furthermore, each response in itself is implicitly addressed to more than one potential receiver and may receive replies from more than one source. In online communities this is further complicated by the absence of turn-taking. (Megele, 2014a)

Turn-taking and a clear topical focus are central to coherent conversations in face-to-face communication, and coherence of communication is central to understanding and effective learning (Herring, 1999). Therefore, the suspension of the turn-taking norms in multilogue communications such as conversations in communities of practice and computer-mediated communications offers unique challenges and opportunities. For example, it allows a broader range of participants to contribute simultaneously to the conversation and to develop multiple lines of thought and threads of discussion that emerge, diverge, and re-merge to form a broader and richer conversation. This dynamic exchange, combined with the 'relative permanence' of online posts as textual or visual artefacts, enables individual participants to speak 'at the same time' and yet to be 'heard' distinctly (Shank, 1993; Megele, 2014a).

In this sense, multilogues generate a less structured and more flexible conversation that allows for an increased number of voices and participants, while broadening the scope of discussion and generating more creative outcomes. Therefore, multilogue conversations can be a powerful tool for brainstorming, idea generation, idea development and other activities that may benefit from a wider engagement and broadening of communication base. Furthermore, participation in interactive online discussions and multilogue conversations such as a Twitter chat can enhance the participants' cognitive ability for sifting through a rapid flux of information and engaging in coherent multilogue conversations (Megele, 2014a).

Locating @SWSCmedia on the continuum between social networks and online communities

The concepts of 'community' and 'network' are often used interchangeably and undifferentiated (Conway and Steward, 1998). However, some authors such as Brown and Duguid (2000) have differentiated the two concepts, distinguishing 'communities of practice' from 'networks of practice', arguing that, the former 'are cohesive groups of people working together on similar tasks', while the latter 'are made of people working on a similar practice who don't necessarily know each other' (Tuomi, 2003, p 127).

@SWSCmedia demonstrates that communities of practice go beyond a network of connection; indeed, we can consider networks and communities as the extremes of a continuum of different possible relations, between the individuals/agents and the environment in which they operate and where a common obligation is central to community and its dynamics (Postman,

1993). The common obligation and adherence to social work values and principles underpinned all engagements and activities of @SWSCmedia.

Although the idea of a common obligation enhances the integrity and cohesion within a community, it also raises the question of whether such an obligation generates a hierarchy and whether that means that communities are necessarily governed by hierarchies.

Lam (2000, 2002) argues that the governance form of a community is located somewhere midway along the continuum between hierarchy and network. Hence, based on Lam's terminology, thinking of community as a common obligation brings the concept of community closer to hierarchy than network (Dal Fiore, 2007). Aware of this embedded nature of hierarchy within all communities, the founder of @SWSCmedia minimised interactions between her personal social media presence and the @SWSCmedia community to ensure that @SWSCmedia remained an open and faceless space that reflected the faces and the voices of its participants.

Dal Fiore's 'Communities versus networks: The implications on innovation and social change' (2007, p 861), describing the characteristics of communities and social networks, states that, whereas the driving force of communities is to maximise social control over the individual and individuality, the driving force of networks is to maximise individual agency and to gain control on sociality. Hence, communities are closed entities requiring conformism to a central obligation and to social rules and roles in exchange for a 'subjectivity' and a sense of belonging to and association with a collective identity; networks are ad hoc and combining containers with fewer barriers to entry, and are exploited by individuals/agents for individualistic purposes and for discovering their self-potential through comparison with other individuals/agents (see Megele with Buzzi, 2017). The central obligation in the @SWSCmedia community was that of evidencing, sharing and strengthening social work narratives, values and ethics alongside practice wisdom and the lived experience of practitioners and people who access services.

Drawing from this thesis, communities are naturally positioned toward assimilation, cultural exchange, conservation and increasing specialisation, whereas networks hold greater potential for evolution (through combination) and increasing differentiation. In other words, communities offer stronger bonds but also regulate their membership more closely; networks allow greater degree of freedom but offer weaker bonds. Distinguishing communities from networks at the extremes of a continuum along the same line of reference allows us to conceptualise infinitely different hybrid derivatives represented in various forms, similar to the ones given in the 'real' world, along that axis (Dal Fiore, 2007; Megele with Buzzi, 2017).

Based on this definition, it can be argued that online communities are more than points of unrestrained cultural encounters and provide more than a 'centre' for cultural exchange. Instead, they are active and dynamic socio-cultural organisms that 'regulate' and 'normalise' groups and individuals and also 'command' conformity to a common set of formal and symbolic expressions (language) and a set of shared meanings (culture) in consonance with their own culture and collective identities within a 'hyperspace' of 'hyper-temporal' 'reality'. Communities therefore, require de facto acculturation of their members through assimilation of their culture and association with their identity (Buzzi and Megele, 2011; Megele with Buzzi, 2017). This implies that, in order to become a part of a community and belong to that community, one should adopt the language (that is, the shared symbolic expressions) and the culture (that is, the shared meaning and values) of that community; this involves acculturation of individuals into a community. Professions and professional organisations regulate their memberships and demand adherence to specific codes of conduct and, hence, offer a basis for the formation of professional communities which in turn reinforce and promote the values and collective identity of that profession.

Communities of practice and professional identity

The process of identity construction lies at the heart of professional development in social work. However, the development, adaptation and enhancement of professional identity involve complex and multi-layered developmental processes and require a recognition of 'the person within the developing professional' (Jack and Donnellan, 2010). @SWSCmedia contributed to professional development and enhancement of professional identity of its participants (Megele, 2014b). These processes can be facilitated through a sense of belonging combined with self-disclosure and discovery in interpersonal and intrapersonal (reflexive) conversations that are often a feature of 'communities of practice' (Wenger, 1998). The @SWSCmedia community, and other online communities such as the @MHChat community, are examples of how such developmental processes can be facilitated through a sense of belonging and professional trust in a reflective space sustained by the online community and its participants. This highlights the opportunity and the need for professional networks and communities of practice that offer a positive context for effective learning and support through reflective sharing of experiences and building a sense of shared 'belonging' (Megele with Buzzi, 2017).

The dynamics of the @SWSCmedia community demonstrate that identity processes in communities of practice are coproductive processes: the collective identity is shaped *by* the identities of its members while at the same time shaping the identity *of* its members. In other words, through engaging in communities of practice, participants develop a shared 'repertoire' (Wenger, 1998, p 153) of knowledge, values, meanings and practices that both define and reinforce the community. In this sense, communities of practice can offer a positive, contained and containing environment that balances validation with regulation through assimilation and that supports the growth and development of the profession and of practitioners' identities and practices (Buzzi, 2020; Buzzi and Megele, 2020).

Therefore, notwithstanding the importance of a 'formalised' agenda and explicit, expressed, and encoded knowledge in communities of practice, the preceding notion of communities of practice goes beyond such considerations and the notion of explicit professional knowledge, to acknowledge the emotional, psychological, psychosocial and phenomenological dimensions of the transitional experiences of practitioners (Buzzi, 2020; Buzzi and Megele, 2020).

The currency of 'doing' over 'being' and the 'explicit' over the 'embodied' is the by-product of the reactionist and 'managerialist' culture that confounds output with outcome and emphasises performance divorced from its emotional labour and outcome divorced from its processes. However, communities of practice recognise and celebrate the physical with psychological, psychosocial and phenomenological dimensions of practice. They offer a validating and yet assimilating environment that enables practitioners to engage in dynamic, unstructured and creative conversations and identity work, and serve as a respite from 'doing' and 'knowing' to engage in 'being' and reflective 'unknowing' and self-discovery, where the tacit become explicit and then embodied in practice (Buzzi, 2020; Buzzi and Megele, 2020).

Furthermore, by tracing and evidencing the ideas, narratives, lived experiences and values of practitioners and people who access services, online communities of practice can generate shared understanding while strengthening the voice and identity of the profession and professionals as well as the people who access services.

Conclusion

Social media users – whether individuals, groups or organisations – aim to create a community around their own identity and interest. In that sense, every social worker using social media has their own personal community of interest or practice, be it a large or a small community of people which can be referred to as the person's Personal Learning Network (PLN). However, creating, developing and supporting a large-scale, leaderful and coproduced community of practice such as @SWSCmedia is a labour of love that requires a staunch dedication to a higher cause and infinite hours of effort and invisible and unrecognised labour.

Communities of practice and communities of interest offer rich and powerful opportunities for personal and professional learning, practice and identity development. Therefore, drawing on research, and the authors' work and experiences of creating several communities of practice/interest as well as knowledge hubs for local government, charities, and the private sector, below are some considerations that may be helpful for creating and developing an online community. These suggestions apply to most types of online communities, be it a large community of practice or community of interest or a community made of friends and social media followers built around an individual's identity or social media account:

- Research indicates (Krasnova et al, 2013) that social media can induce envy and narcissism and can lead to bullying behaviour. A few months after starting @SWSCmedia chats, the first author experienced trolling and significant bullying from some of the most unexpected sources. These situations are always complex and difficult to manage and one is often overcome by fear. Hiding from the trolling and bullying only emboldened the bullies and took its toll on the first author. Eventually the bullies began directing their aggression toward the most active members of @SWSCmedia community; this resulted in some members avoiding the chats while others closed their accounts and withdrew from social media altogether. Upon reflection and with the benefit of hindsight, the first author concludes she should have stood firm and spoken up against the bullies, whose intention was '… to destroy the good in the other' (Payton, 2007). There are no fixed solutions or answers for addressing such behaviours and concerns, but it is important to have a clear and consistent policy and the required support, time and capacity to process and manage the challenges that arise and to respond in a contextually relevant, appropriate and proportionate manner.
- Shared values, principles and ethics and a common area of engagement and interest, as well as clear objectives and strategy, are foundational to communities of practice and interest.
- Creating social work or other professional communities of practice and interest requires a strong sense of identify tempered with humility and enriched with reflection and professional curiosity to ensure a purposeful and yet open, inclusive and explorative attitude (Megele with Buzzi, 2017).

- Many people choose to build a community around their own identity; however, the creation of a separate social media account was important and symbolised a number of different things; most importantly, that the @SWSCmedia community was about ideas, ideals and values, rather than a given individual or group of individuals, and that it had its own identity. Given that human interactions are never neutral, this point requires constant and consistent attention, reflection and action.
- Problems and challenges can come from the most unexpected sources and when least expected. Therefore, it is important to have a clear and consistent policy for managing trolling, aggression and abuse, and to address inappropriate behaviour be it passive aggressive or overt aggression.
- Coproductive opportunities and a sense of community and co-ownership of ideas, initiatives and actions are central and of great importance to communities of practice; that is, it is important that the community takes ownership of itself and is owned by its members rather than being owned by an individual. In the case of @SWSCmedia this was put into practice in several ways: for example, those who were willing and actively engaged in the @SWSCmedia community could tweet, moderate and engage in facilitating the community's activities while maintaining the focus on the community rather than the individual.
- Although engaging community members and volunteers in facilitating community's activities is very positive, to ensure adherence to professional codes of ethics such volunteers need support, training and supervision. In the initial phases, this requires significant additional time with no certainty that volunteers will be able to continue sharing their time with the community.
- @SWSCmedia created an open access community and resource for discussion, knowledge generation, and identity formation among social workers; this was in line with its objective of providing a counternarrative by evidencing and promoting good practice. However, in creating a new community, it is important to carefully consider and decide whether an open access or closed community can better serve the purposes of the community and its members.

- @SWSCmedia's strategy was to depersonalise the community, allowing it to be many different things for different people; as such, it offered a faceless community of many faces (where no single voice dominates and where everyone has a voice, place, and space and can speak and be heard). This is empowering for participants and cultivates professional leadership and leaderful practice. However, given that human interactions and relationships are never neutral, the objective of creating and maintaining a faceless community, which projects the faces of its members and offers a space and a 'blank sheet' for each participant to write their own narratives, is an inspirational as well as aspirational goal that requires constant and consistent attention, reflection and action. Furthermore, the openly accommodating and faceless nature of such a community may also be perceived as a vacuum or a gap in the community and/or its ownership that may be exploited by others. For example, one of the community members of @SWSCmedia published an article in a student magazine falsely claiming to be the creator and the person behind @SWSCmedia.
- @SWSCmedia created a constructively critical public space to discuss and debate social work practice and education and other related topics during a time when many social workers felt unconfident and uncertain about social media use. However, social media is an open and unregulated space; at times, discussions can be affected and skewed by one or more people who may confuse negativity with being critical or who may use confrontational language and aggression as a strategy for attention or for dominating the community space. Such individuals are toxic for communities: the community and its members should have the maturity, strength of identity and values, and courage to challenge such behaviours and attitudes.

Although the combination of ideas with individual passion is a necessary starting point for thinking about or starting a community of practice or a community of interest, the success and continuation of such communities is a complex process that requires thoughtful planning and mindful and consistent dedication; it also entails considerable sacrifice, often accompanied by endless hours of unacknowledged, invisible and faceless labour for a higher cause and without assurances of success or a desired outcome. However, communities of practice/interest offer unlimited opportunities for learning, identity formation and personal and professional development – and a priceless sense of contributing toward a greater cause.

Most importantly, rather than a status or state of being communities of practice are in constant state of becoming. In other words, rather than being a point of arrival or a destination, communities of practice and their dynamics, ideals and objectives are a journey of sharing, learning and of giving of self to support others' personal and professional development and growth that needs to be lived and appreciated in its here and now while maintaining a vision and high aspirations with an eye to the future.

References

Brown, J. S. and Duguid, P. (2000) *The Social Life of Information*. Boston: Harvard Business School.

Buzzi, P. (2020) *Relationship based Practice in Digital Age*. London: PSW Network.

Buzzi, P. and Megele, C. (2011) 'Cyber-communities and motherhood online – a reflection on transnational adoption' in M. Moravec (ed) *Motherhood Online*, Cambridge: Cambridge Scholars Publishing.

Buzzi, P. and Megele, C. (2020) *Digital Practice and Working with Children and Young People Online*. London: PSW Network.

Conway, S. and Steward, F. (1998) 'Mapping innovation networks', *International Journal of Innovation Management*, 2(2): 223–54.

Dal Fiore, F. (2007) 'Communities versus networks: The implications on innovation and social change', *American Behavioral Science*, 50(7): 857–66.

Dane, E. and Pratt, M. G. (2007) 'Exploring intuition and its role in managerial decision making', *Academy of Management Review*, 32(1): 33–54.

Dominowski, R. L. and Dallob, P. (1995) 'Insight and problem solving', in R. J. Sternberg and J. E. Davidson (eds), *The Nature of Insight* (pp 33–62). Cambridge, MA: MIT Press.

Gergen, K. J. (1991) *The Saturated Self: Dilemmas of identity in contemporary life*. New York: Basic Books.

Herring, S. (1999) 'Interactional coherence in CMC', *Journal of Computer Mediated Communication*, 4(4). Available at: https://onlinelibrary.wiley.com/doi/full/10.1111/j.1083-6101.1999.tb00106.x

Jack, G. and Donnellan, H. (2010) 'Recognising the person within the developing professional: Tracking the early careers of newly qualified child care social workers in three local authorities in England', *Social Work Education*, 29(3): 305–18.

Jones, R. (2012) 'Child protection, social work and the media: doing as well as being done to', *Research, Policy and Planning*, 29(2): 83–94.

Krasnova, H., Wenninger, H., Widjaja, T. and Buxmann, P. (2013) 'Envy on Facebook: A hidden threat to users' life satisfaction?' *Wirtschaftsinformatik Proceedings 2013* 92. Available at: http://aisel.aisnet.org/wi2013/92

Lam, A. (2000) 'Tacit knowledge, organizational learning and societal institutions: An integrated framework', *Organizational Studies*, 21(3): 487–513.

Lam, A. (2002) 'Alternative societal models of learning and innovation in the knowledge economy', *International Social Science Journal*, 54(171): 67–82.

Megele, C. (2014a) 'Theorizing Twitter chat', *Journal of Perspectives in Applied Academic Practice*, 2(2). Available at: http://jpaap.napier.ac.uk/index.php/JPAAP/article/view/106/html

Megele, C. (2014b) 'eABLE: Embedding social media in academic curriculum as a learning and assessment strategy to enhance students learning and e-professionalism', *Innovations in Education and Teaching International*, 52(4): 414–25.

Megele, C. (2015) 'e-Learning and Blended Learning: Embedding social media in academic curricula: exploring technology, enquiry and pedagogy'. Higher Education Academy. Available at: https://prezi.com/w8o7fz3ukver/social-media-elearning-blended-learning/

Megele, C. with Buzzi, P. (2017) *Safeguarding Children and Young People Online*. Bristol: Policy Press.

Payton, C. (2007) 'Envy: The canker in the bud', *Psychodynamic Practice*, 13(2): 183–95.

Postman, N. (1993) *Technopoly: The surrender of culture to technology*. New York: Vintage.
Shank, G. (1993) 'Abductive multiloguing: The semiotic dynamics of navigating the Net', *Arachnet Electronic Journal on Virtual Culture*, 1(01).
Tuomi, I. (2003) *Networks of Innovation: Change and meaning in the age of the Internet*. Oxford: Oxford University Press.
Wenger, E. (1998) *Communities of Practice: Learning, meaning, and identity*. Cambridge: Cambridge University Press.

8

Social media and social work regulation

Claudia Megele, Lyn Romeo and Peter Buzzi

Introduction

The effective regulation of professionalism and digital practice in an increasingly mediated world, one dominated by a rapidly changing socio-technological, cultural and practice landscape, presents significant and evolving challenges and opportunities spanning from frontline practice to strategic management of services and from education to employment and regulation of social work. However, the notion of digital practice in social work is relatively new; indeed, it was only in 2012 when for the first time in social work, Megele (2012) used and defined the terms e-professionalism and digital professionalism in social work and social care. Eight years may not seem very long, but in social media terms it represents a relatively long time, with significant changes in technology over that period. In December 2012, a working group from the British Association of Social Workers (BASW) produced BASW's first social media policy with the following purpose:

> The purpose of this policy is to clarify what BASW considers to be the professional responsibilities of

> social workers and social work students, in relation to the increasing use of social media. As a professional body across the UK, BASW has developed a policy to support members to use social media appropriately and ensure practice is based on the BASW Code of Ethics. (BASW, 2012a)

This was an important step at the time and already within that policy BASW recognised the importance of e-professionalism and digital professionalism in social work:

> One of the key messages to emerge from developing the policy is the need for all social workers to be 'e-professionals', a term used particularly by one of our group, Claudia Megele. It involves the ability to understand and use social media, as well as how to develop and manage it for networking, communication, CPD and developing inclusive practice. (BASW, 2012b)

Since then, there have been significant changes in technology, society and social work practice and subsequently the authors (Megele with Buzzi, 2017; Megele, 2014, 2018) and a number of other authors have written about e-professionalism and digital professionalism, while both practitioners and regulators have faced new and changing practical and ethical decisions and challenges in relation to digital practice and safeguarding of people who access social work services.

So far this book has discussed some of the applications and implications of social media in social work practice and education, including ethics of social media and the question of e-professionalism and digital professionalism in Chapter 2. This chapter examines some of the professional and regulatory challenges and opportunities associated with social workers' use of social media and their changing role as digital practitioners. It begins by examining the changing landscape and service users' changing expectations, followed by a discussion of professionalism and power imbalance between practitioner and service user and how social media may mitigate this imbalance. This is followed by a discussion of the need for complementing the current principle-based approach to regulation with a more systemic and behavioural approach. The authors then draw on current legislation and guidance to address the question of whether social workers can search, view and monitor service users' social media accounts and online behaviours, followed by messages from research regarding social workers' use of social media and viewing of service users' social media posts. The chapter then examines the learning from two HCPC fitness to practise hearings and concludes with some mindlines for professional practice and regulation in social work.

This chapter follows on from Chapter 2, and it may be helpful to read Chapter 2 first.

Social media and social work: the changing landscape and expectations

Social work has been rather slow in recognising the impact and importance of digital and social media technologies in practice and the changing expectations of people who access social work and social care services. Indeed, Buzzi and Megele (2020) – investigating the preferences of young people and their families and carers using semi-structured phone interviews combined with focus groups involving young people and their families and carers – found that young people and their families would like practitioners to liaise with them through multiple communication channels, including social media, text and email, and that such flexible use of digital and social media technologies can generate and sustain feelings of closeness and caring. As relationship-based practitioners, social workers should go beyond 'copresence' and establish a sense of others and a psychological connection with the other that allows a sharing of thoughts and feelings combined with a sense of having access to another person's mental states (that is, their thoughts, intentions and affects) (Megele, 2015). Social media and the increasing social presence can generate a sense of closeness and projected sense of access to another person's thoughts, intentions and affect (Suler, 2004; LaMendola, 2010; Buzzi and Megele,

2012). Indeed, young people and their families and carers expressed frustration with practitioners' and services' insistence on traditional channels of engagement such as the phone and home visits. Buzzi and Megele's (2020) findings indicate that practitioners found home visits to be infrequent and driven by practitioners' and services' needs for information gathering rather than service users' need for support. Furthermore, research participants found it cumbersome and frustrating to have to go through centralised phone lines and switchboard operators in order to contact their social worker and/or services; this contributed to a perception of the inaccessibility and/or unavailability of practitioners and/or services. Most young people and the majority of parents and carers expected flexible communication on the part of practitioners and services, and there was a correlation between ease of communication with practitioners plus timeliness of response from practitioners and services and the service users' satisfaction and positive perception of services.

Meeting service users' expectations of flexibility of communication requires practitioners to use social media and communication technologies to establish and maintain a positive social and online presence and to engage positively with service users for professional purposes. However, these expectations are not reflected in social media guidance and policies in most local authorities. Having said that, there are a number of excellent and innovative projects and initiatives by local authorities using digital and social media technologies. Some examples include: Hampshire County Council as well as other adult social care services' use of Amazon's Echo and Alexa AI technology to provide virtual assistance and support for older people; Salford City Council began an initiative to enhance the digital citizenship of 8,000 'digitally excluded' residents in their city (Clark, 2017); and some councils are beginning to use AI and big data in more creative ways to enhance practice and services; however, there are both positive and negative outcomes associated with use of AI (Buzzi, 2020a, 2020b).

Working Together to Safeguard Children (HM Government, 2018) is the first piece of social work guidance that recognises the need to enhance social workers' knowledge and skills in this area. It states that, 'To be effective, practitioners need to continue to develop their knowledge and skills in this area and be aware of the new and emerging threats, including online abuse, grooming, sexual exploitation and radicalisation' (HM Government, 2018: pp 12–13). BASW's revised Professional Capabilities Framework (PCF) refers to '… using social media positively' and being able to '… apply research theory, evidence and knowledge from social work and other relevant fields (for example, sociology, … technological and digital spheres…) to social work practice'. Nonetheless, unfortunately neither of these takes adequate notice of the changing practice landscape nor offers a clear pathway for developing practitioners' knowledge and skill in this area, nor do they address some of the more complex and challenging ethical and practical difficulties faced by practitioners in everyday practice. An example of a question that requires further clarity and statutory guidance is whether practitioners should use Google search to gather information about service users and whether they should include such information as evidence in assessments or reports (for example, court reports) and safeguarding plans.

This chapter addresses this question later. Given the changing practice and regulatory landscape, the remainder of this chapter highlights some of the challenges relating to digital practice and professional regulation of social work.

Mitigating the power imbalance between professionals and service users

Professional regulations define and structure the relationships between professions and professionals in relation to the state, society, other professions and occupations, the public, and the people who access the services of that profession and its professionals. Clark (1995: p 15) defines status as 'the power to solicit respect'. Weber (1978) explains that professions are status groups: their professional status groups emerge when people and occupations share a position of privilege and social esteem and this status serves as the basis for a profession's claim and monopoly of a given area of practice. Both the protected nature of the title of 'social worker' and social workers' adherence to social work values and a professional code of ethics underpin social work professionalism and define social work as a profession. However, given social work's principle of empowerment and anti-discriminatory, anti-oppressive practice, although professional identity and status have been central to the study of professions, the challenge for social work is to mitigate and minimise the power difference between practitioners and people who access services while maintaining the status and integrity of the profession.

The use of social media technologies to communicate with service users can mitigate some of this power imbalance. Indeed, given the multilogue (many-to-many) and unstructured nature of online communication, it is often difficult – if not impossible – for one party to control the online exchange and communication (see Megele, 2014 for a more detailed explanation of multilogue and online communication and its implications). This mitigates the power imbalance inherent in human interactions and, in practice, requires practitioners to relinquish some of the control and power that they usually hold over communication and encounters with people who access services. For example, as highlighted in Chapter 3, a new protocol designed for gathering the views of young people in care enables young people to share their thoughts, feelings and everyday experiences over time and serves as a valuable resource for planning and decision making, including care planning and review meetings. Initial feedback suggests that young people appreciate such approaches and protocols and find these engagements more suited to their needs; this supports relationship-based practice and enhances the sense of closeness and continuity of service as well as the practitioner's availability and caring. Furthermore, the data gathered through such approaches offer a much richer and better view of the young person's experiences over time and can complement the face-to-face meetings with practitioners or for review of care plans.

Routine adoption of such approaches represents a major change in social work practice and raises new ethical and boundary challenges for practitioners and regulators that require a dynamic and forward-looking regulatory perspective.

Regulation and professionalism: the need for a behavioural and systemic view

Regulatory guidance and professional ethics and values underpin professionalism and the professional regulation of social work and, although professionalism may not be sufficient to achieve the profound and far-reaching changes needed in social care, without it, the social work profession, practice and services are lost. There is a strong need for a clear and practice-based definition of professionalism that includes e-professionalism or digital professionalism and digital citizenship. However, most policies and guidance defining professionalism in social work are principle-based and relatively abstract. Notwithstanding the importance of professionalism, given the complexity of the social media landscape it is essential that such policies and regulation are complemented by behavioural examples, guidance and a systemic perspective to clearly outline what professional behaviour looks like in practice, as well as how digital and social media technologies influence practice and professionalism in social work and social care. The combination of principle-based, systemic and behavioural approaches to regulation and professionalism makes the pursuit of professionalism more visible, accessible and attainable in everyday practice.

From a regulatory perspective this also implies that regulators should consider the changing practice landscape and its impact on communication, behaviours, relationships and expectations. This challenges regulators, policy makers and legislators to adopt a systemic perspective and to move away from categorical and generalised statements regarding digital practice and online activities and instead offer a much more nuanced and sophisticated and practice-based sense of ethics and professionalism in social work.

Furthermore, as suggested by the definition of e-professionalism or digital professionalism in Chapter 2 and from a systemic perspective, professionalism and professional expectations and behaviours are profoundly influenced by the organisational and environmental context of social work practice. Therefore, it is essential that social work regulation should require employers and organisational leaders to ensure that organisational and environmental variables and contexts promote, enable and support – rather than inhibit – professionalism in practice. This implies that fitness for practice investigations should also examine the organisational and environmental factors and context that led to a situation or outcome that required regulatory intervention and the investigation. Such an approach to professionalism offers the opportunity to improve practice and services through education and continuous learning and through system-level reform. Indeed, professionalism requires firsthand experience and learning and is a capacity that can be developed over time. Furthermore, conceptualising professionalism as a set of behaviours, supported by a specific set of skills and competencies, challenges the traditional notion of professionalism as an attitudinal competency or character traits and instead offers a path to professionalism based on an experiential and explicit learning and development model.

In particular, the systemic view invites practitioners and regulators to consider the layered and complex nature of social work practice and both online and offline relationships and how these are impacted by social technologies. This includes awareness and understanding of the increasing impact of the modes and dimensions of social presence and the visibility of online behaviour, digital convergence, digilanguage, blurring of online boundaries and new forms and dimensions of dual relationships (see Chapter 2 for a more detailed discussion of these elements).

Accessing service users' social media accounts or online data information

---

Example: The case of Peter Connelly

After the tragic death of baby Peter Connelly at the hands of his mother, Tracy, and her new boyfriend Steven Barker, certain media outlets questioned why the social workers did not examine the mother's Facebook activity. These questions were subsequent to emerging information about the mother's public Facebook posts that explicitly evidenced her relationship with her partner. *The Guardian* reported that

Tracy regularly shared information about herself on social media showing that, instead of looking after and nurturing her son, she spent her days 'drinking vodka, watching pornographic films, and having sex' with Steven Barker. She also posted 'Madly in love with the most amazing guy' (*Guardian*, 2009) and that her 'fella is nuts' (*Guardian*, 2009). Given that professionals and social services were unaware of the mother's lifestyle and the presence of her boyfriend in the house, knowledge of such social media posts could have helped professionals recognise the unsuitability of Peter's home environment and his mother's behaviour. Potentially, this information could have resulted in a more assertive action by services and possibly saved Peter's life.

Given the abundance of readily available data and information about people online, the case of Peter Connelly (see example box) and other similar situations raise the question of whether, as part of their information gathering, social workers should conduct social media searches and/or access or view service users' online profiles, digital postings or other online activities. Should social workers Google service users and should they use and consider the Google search results in their assessments and safeguarding plans? Should employers provide practitioners with social media accounts to serve and support people who access services? Should social workers monitor service users' social media activities or posts if they think children or vulnerable adults are at risk of harm and such information may help their assessments or safeguarding plans and/or may mitigate risk of harm?

The Regulation of Investigatory Powers Act 2000 (RIPA) provides guidance with regards to surveillance and use of investigatory powers invested in relevant public authorities. However, RIPA applies to activities or offences that carry a minimum of six-month custodial sentence, and most social work assessments and reports do not entail six months custodial sentence and therefore cannot obtain RIPA authorisation. In 2016, the Office of Surveillance Commissioners provided more explicit guidance with regards to searching, accessing, viewing or using online data and communication by a member of public authority. This guidance (OSC, 2016) offers some very important and helpful clarifications regarding the use of online data and communication that can be applied to social work. In summary, some of the more salient and relevant points for social work practice and regulation are:

- The Human Rights Act 1998 requires the council, its representatives, and organisations working on its behalf, pursuant to Article 8 of the European Convention, to respect the private and family life of citizens, their home and their correspondence.
- Private information under RIPA includes: 'any information relating to a person's private or family life and should be taken generally to include any aspect of a person's private or personal relationships with others, including family and professional or business relationships'.
- Practitioners should not use their personal social media account to access, view or gather information involving service users' social media account or online activities.
- 'The fact that digital investigation is routine or easy to conduct does not reduce the need for authorisation. Care must be taken to understand how the SNS being used works.'
- The onus for privacy rests with the individual or organisation posting or sharing the information. However, although the data/information may be in public domain, 'it is unwise to regard it as – open source, or publicly available; the author has a reasonable expectation of privacy if access controls are applied.'
- 'Where privacy settings are available but not applied the data may be considered open source and an authorisation is not usually required.' This defines the meaning of open source data and although it suggests that access to such data is not unlawful, it should be read in conjunction with the notion of surveillance as defined in the next point.
- 'Repeat viewing of – open source sites may constitute directed surveillance on a case by case basis and this should be borne in mind.'
- '... if it is necessary and proportionate for a public authority to covertly breach access controls, the minimum requirement is an authorisation for directed surveillance. An

authorisation for the use and conduct of a CHIS [Covert Human Intelligence Sources] is necessary if a relationship is established or maintained by a member of a public authority or by a person acting on its behalf (that is, the activity is more than mere reading of the site's content).' This would be the case if a social worker used an anonymous social media account to connect with a service user.

- 'It is not unlawful for a member of a public authority to set up a false identity but it is inadvisable for a member of a public authority to do so for a covert purpose without an authorisation for directed surveillance when private information is likely to be obtained.' (Quotations are from OSC, 2016)

The preceding two points about CHIS and authorisation for directed surveillance state that practitioners should never use fake or anonymous social media accounts to access or view service users' data on social media and that such actions require authorisation for directed surveillance. However, as mentioned earlier, RIPA authorisation cannot be obtained for most social work cases since the minimum requirement for obtaining RIPA authorisation or authorisation for directed surveillance is that the investigation should involve an offence with a minimum of six-month custodial sentence.

The points listed clarify a number of important practice-related challenges and highlight some of the current legal guidance. However, it is important to note that social work is a relationship-based profession; in addition to ensuring actions and decisions are *lawful*, social workers should consider and ensure that their actions and decisions are *ethical* and in line with social work values and ethics. Current ethical guidance suggests that it is not appropriate for social workers to conduct overt or covert surveillance of service users either online or offline. Tools such as SMART mapping and the 10 Cs risk and resilience toolkit (see Chapter 2) offer collaborative approaches for working with children and young people and adult service users. Megele with Buzzi (2017) and Buzzi and Megele (2020) have developed a motivational language and approach for the use of SMART mapping and the 10 Cs in direct work with young people. These are non-intrusive and relationship-based approaches that raise young people's awareness and promote shared understanding while enabling practitioners to understand young people's motivations, how and why they use social media, and their understanding of online risks, benefits and privacy as well as appropriate and inappropriate behaviours online. Such approaches ensure better informed and systemic assessment of online risks and build trust and better relationships that are the foundation of holistic and effective safeguarding of young people and adult service users both online and offline.

Furthermore, even when the information is received in a lawful and ethical manner, practitioners should be aware of the complexities around authenticating online information and verifying its reliability. Screenshots and printouts can be manipulated by editing the information, so practitioners should clarify the information source and trail and be clear about how and where the information was found. These verifications do not imply that the information in question necessarily constitutes admissible evidence in court. Sarah's experience as described in the following case example emphasises the question of admissibility of information.

Example: admissibility and consent

Sarah is the mother of two young children and has been the target of domestic abuse by her partner. In a home visit, Sarah showed her social worker private social media messages from her partner threatening Sarah. The social worker included this information in her court statement. As a result, the judge asked Sarah if she was happy for this information to be admitted in court. In this case, the mother wanted the information to be considered by the court and was happy to give consent.

This example highlights that, although Sarah had volunteered this information and shared it with her social worker, its admissibility in court was subject to her explicit consent. Although the communication was private between her and her partner, Sarah was a party to the communication and therefore in a position to offer consent and disclose the content of that communication to the Court. Therefore, when thinking about searching social media data and using online information in social work assessments or reports, practitioners should consider whether their actions and decisions are lawful, proportionate, ethical and in line with social work values, and whether they are clear about the authenticity, reliability and the trail of how the information was obtained. Finally, they should consider the admissibility of the information.

Practitioners work with unverified information every day and should assess social media information as they would any other. This means information received through other sources (for example, partners or neighbours) and taken from social media or online sources require the same due diligence with which practitioners handle and assess offline or verbal information or allegations. If in doubt, practitioners should seek advice from their manager and appropriate legal guidance and practice guidance within their organisation.

Messages from research about of social work's accessing service users' social media information and the changing service user expectations

The preceding section clarifies a number of important points in relation to practitioners accessing and viewing service users' data and information on social media; it also provides greater clarity around surveillance, open source data and so on. There is precious limited research in this area, and most such research is small scale and involves limited number of participants and hence is not representative. However, the recent national research and practice development project provides valuable and nationally representative evidence in digital professionalism and online safeguarding. The preliminary findings from this research underline the lack of clarity among practitioners and in current guidance with regards to social workers' access and use of service users' social media data and activities (Buzzi, 2019). This underscores the need for more explicit regulatory guidance to raise awareness and ensure clarity of the standards of good practice.

For example, Sage and Sage (2016) carried out an online survey involving 171 child welfare workers to study the use of social media in child welfare practice in the US. They found that 94 (55%) respondents thought that it was acceptable to search for information on service users via social media out of curiosity, at least in some situations; 73 respondents (43%) had actually done so, while 86 respondents (50%) reported their colleagues had done so. 'Respondents reported greater acceptability and frequency' of such searches when they were work related (for example, locating a missing service user or contacting relatives). Twelve respondents (7%) reported that their colleagues had 'accepted or initiated an online friend request from a client'. Thirty respondents (18%) 'reported that their colleagues have created fake profiles to gain access to client information'. Twenty-four respondents (14%) 'reported that they have used social media to vent about their workdays' (p 102). Similar concerning behaviours and breaches of social work practice standards have been evidenced in the UK (Turner, 2019) although in a smaller proportion relative to the US. These challenges offer important points for reflection and consideration for practitioners and regulators.

In a different study, Breyette and Hill found that respondents used social media to monitor the activities of their service users online and believed that this was justified since those social media profiles were public (2015, p 300). These studies demonstrate some of the ways in which practitioners are using social media in practice and reveal a number of questionable uses of social media that infringe on the privacy of service users, either out of curiosity or out of other practice-related motivations.

Gathering social workers' views about use of social media in practice and involving 232 children and families social workers in UK, Buzzi and Megele (2020) found that about 45% of respondents thought it would be OK to check service users social media accounts for child protection purposes and about 22% of respondents had checked service users' social media profiles.

Such findings highlight the need for much greater awareness and education, and much more explicit, systemic and behavioural guidance and regulation. Furthermore, Buzzi and Megele found that 9 in 10 practitioners did not routinely consider young people's use of social media in their assessments and reports unless there were specific concerns around their usage. Given the role and significance of social media in young people's lives, relationships and identity and the amount of time they spend online, lack of systematic and ethical consideration of online risks in social work assessments (both in terms of potential positive or negative outcomes) is tantamount to ignoring a significant amount of young people's everyday experiences and the activities, behaviours and relationships that are of primary importance to them and that have a significant impact on their identity, self-esteem and wellbeing as well as personal and social development (Polignano et al, 2017; Buzzi, 2020c; Buzzi and Megele, 2020). It is essential that social work guidance and regulation should consider the ethical and practical implications and applications of digital and social media technologies in social work practice and safeguarding in terms of the new and changing landscape and expectations, new and changing standards of good practice and due diligence, new and changing personal and professional boundaries, and so on.

Consistently exhibiting professionalism is a practised skill that goes beyond 'knowing right from wrong' or having a strong 'internal compass'. It involves evidence-informed analysis and reflective critical perspective with a focus on the best outcomes for and interests of people who access services. Regulation and regulators play a key role in this area; they lay the foundation for good, ethical practice and, therefore, should explicitly address these and other similar questions that challenge practitioners on a daily basis. Such an approach to professionalism and professional regulation is both behavioural and developmental and highlights that challenges to demonstrating professionalism in practice are routine, not anomalous. Development of professional competency should focus on building practitioners' knowledge, skills, critical reflection, adaptability and professional resilience to ensure they can respond effectively and resourcefully to ethical challenges.

Practitioners' knowledge of online risks and digital safeguarding

It is also important that social workers are able to guide and support children and young people as well as adults and their families and carers in relation to online/digital risks and safeguarding. It is increasingly evident that restrictive approaches that prohibit social workers and social care practitioners from accessing social media are inadequate and can entail significant repercussions. Such approaches fail to consider the embedded nature of digital and social media technologies in everyday experiences, the powerful and empowering solutions such technologies offer social work, and that unequal access to digital technologies is an increasing source of inequality in society. Given social work's objective of achieving greater equality in society, it is essential that digital access and digital citizenship are an integral part of social work assessments (Megele with Buzzi, 2017; Megele and Buzzi, 2018). There are a number of important initiatives (as described in the next chapter), however, practice has not moved in lock step with these developments. For example, consider the experiences of two concerned mothers seeking advice from social workers about their adopted children being contacted by their birth parents on social media:

> 'When I asked social workers for advice, they just said to monitor her. But it's unrealistic to think that teenagers won't go on Facebook – if only on a friend's phone – in the end, that is exactly what happened.'

> 'In my experience, social workers just aren't technologically savvy and so their advice is basic and unhelpful.'

Such examples are unhelpful for children and families, and they undermine the knowledge, skills and credibility of social work and social workers as digital practitioners. Indeed, lack of appropriate analysis, consideration and planning to safeguard both young and old people who access services and ensure their wellbeing both online and offline may be construed as lack of due diligence in practice. However, e-professionalism and digital professionalism and embedding social media in social work practice require appropriate training and support for social workers and these should be reflected in social work education and employment, and the policies and regulation governing these. The development and implementation of a forward-looking regulatory approach are both a challenge and opportunity for social work and Social Work England as the new regulator for the profession.

The need for more effective use of social media was reflected in the decision of Justice Holman ([2017] EWFC 19), who cancelled an adoption hearing for a 4-year-old because social workers had been unable to trace the birth mother. Justice Holman stated that, in the absence of other channels, professionals should have used Facebook to contact the birth mother and to invite her for the court hearing. It is important to note that Justice Holman's decision was in relation to a very specific context and that it was meant to uphold the mother's rights and interests and to give voice to her views rather than to intrude or infringe upon her rights or gather information about her.

The assessment square or assessment diamond (see Figure 3.1) is an example of an integrated approach to assessing online risks and holistic safeguarding of children and young people both online and offline. Similarly the 10 Cs risk and resilience typologies can be used to assess online risks and to support and safeguard vulnerable adults both online and offline.

In the remainder of this chapter we will draw on the discussion of e-professionalism and digital professionalism from Chapter 2 to highlight some important learnings from the HCPC fitness to practise hearings in relation to digital practice and regulation of social work

Learning from the HCPC fitness to practise hearings

The case example from Chapter 2 in which a social worker shared confidential professional information relating to her case on Facebook accompanied by inappropriate comments offers valuable learning. Indeed, the HCPC statement indicated that: 'The Panel paid close attention to the wording of the paragraph, which referred to putting "at risk the confidentiality of service users", not actually breaching it'. This is an important observation which demonstrates that fitness to practise cases go beyond 'acts of commission' and consider putting 'at risk' and the 'potential' for breach of professional standards. This should be taken into careful consideration when thinking about online posts and digital and social media engagements, their implications and the potential for replication and dissemination of information. Given the circumstances, it is difficult to quantify or demonstrate the precise impact and consequences of the practitioner's online posts and behaviour in this case example. The HCPC panel concluded that the social worker's fitness to practise was impaired and decided to '...impose a Conditions of Practice Order and concluded that a period of 12 months was the proportionate length of time. The Order will be subject to a mandatory review shortly before the expiry of the order.'

Furthermore, it is interesting to note that no consideration seems to have been given by the HCPC to the fact that social worker's Facebook posts were known to her manager and that the social worker's manager had commented on one of the Facebook posts that were the subject of the investigation and found to be inappropriate by the HCPC. Given that her manager had seen the posts, and had even participated in the discussion, does not exonerate the social worker concerned; however, it provides context and evidences her manager's implicit approval of the social worker's behaviour. It suggests that the manager did not see anything wrong with the posting and discussion of the case on social media. Nonetheless, there was no investigation or questioning of the manager's comments, actions or inactions, all of which could have provided a hint for further learning and training for the practitioner and the manager concerned.

This raises a number of important questions that remain unanswered. Given the challenging role of regulation with many grey areas in guidance and legislation, it is important that regulators are fair, clear and transparent in their decision making and ensure that their judgements and decisions are based on a systemic perspective, supported with appropriate evidence, and that motivation and context for their decision are clearly explained.

The decision to suspend the social worker in this case example could be considered as a reaction by the regulator to protect the status and integrity of the profession. However, given the temporary nature of the order and that it was subject to a

12-month review and drawing on restorative principles, it is important that such decisions are accompanied by a clear set of behavioural, competency and capability requirements. These should highlight the knowledge, awareness, skills and capabilities that the practitioner needs to develop and demonstrate, and when possible should serve as a map for the practitioner's restorative journey to eventual re-enablement and reintegration into the profession.

The next case example highlights further important points, including that of anonymity, and the tension between individual freedom of speech and professional responsibility to adhere to professional standards. It should be emphasised that anonymity does not justify aggressive or inappropriate behaviour and that, as a general rule, social workers should ensure that everything they say and do online can stand open scrutiny.

Example: Freedom of speech versus professional responsibility

An experienced social worker was referred to and investigated by the HCPC for inappropriate comments and 'use of obscene' language on Twitter. Using his own personal social media account in his own name, the social worker in question had addressed online posts to the Prime Minister, other politicians and business people.

The HCPC website indicates that these social media posts were made between October 2012 and October 2013. The social worker had indicated that they had 22 followers during this time, three of whom were his personal friends. There were also other posts that did not impact on a professional image.

The social worker told the HCPC panel that he 'bitterly' regretted his actions and explained that he was 'going through a very dark period' when he made those online posts.

The HCPC panel investigating the case concluded that the tweets constituted 'misconduct and/or lack of competence'. The panel concluded that although the social worker's actions constituted 'misconduct', 'the registrant's misconduct was at the lower end of the spectrum of matters that would adversely affect the public's confidence in the profession' , that the social worker's actions had no impact on service users or colleagues, and that there was no evidence of harm to anyone 'including those who were the recipients of the profane tweets'. Therefore, the panel concluded that the social worker's fitness to practise was not impaired and no sanction was warranted.

In this case example, the social worker told the HCPC panel that the 'anonymous environment' of social media platform led him to make comments to individuals 'that he would not dream of making directly to their faces'. This is an interesting and important point: although there are many social workers who use social media anonymously and under pseudonyms, this social worker did not have an anonymous account and was posting under his own name. However, the social worker's statement suggests that he could have been influenced by the online disinhibition effect (Suler, 2004) and cocoon effect Megele with Buzzi, 2017; Megele, 2018; Buzzi, 2019) (see Chapter 2 for a more detailed explanation). The ability to dissociate self from one's online identity and behaviour leads to increased disinhibition online, while the cocoon effect suggests that the social worker's limited number of followers and limited online interactions and replies, combined with the lack of reply from the Prime Minister or other people he was tweeting, may have generated a cocoon effect that led to an imagined sense of invisibility or lack of visibility (that is, the tweets not being noticed by anyone) and anonymity (similar to being unidentifiable or invisible in a crowd): this explains the social worker's statement about Twitter being an 'anonymous environment'. The cocoon effect and this perception of anonymity may have further reinforced the online disinhibition effect, influencing and limiting the social worker's appraisal of the consequences of his behaviour and online posts. This example demonstrates how the cocoon effect can reinforce a given thought, perception, sensation, emotion or feeling or a given action.

Another important issue in this case was the question of civil and individual freedom, rights and liberties, including freedom of speech and expression. The HCPC's statement indicates that,

'It was submitted on the registrant's behalf that his comments were protected by the principle of freedom of speech'.

> These comments reflected the registrant's political beliefs and these tweets were therefore to be given protected status as expressions of these political views. Furthermore, if these tweets were considered offensive there was no rule in law against being rude. (*Community Care*, 11 August 2015)

This assertion with regards to political views should be considered in conjunction with the statement by the Chair of the HCPC panel in an interview saying, 'In adopting offensive language he has demonstrated poor judgment', and that his comments 'have brought the profession into disrepute'. She added, 'A member of the public would regard these … comments to be obscene, offensive and inappropriate for a member of the social worker profession' (*Community Care*, 2015).

Therefore, notwithstanding the individuals' freedom of speech and civil liberties, by accepting to be a registered professional one accepts the values and the professional standards and responsibilities associated with that profession and thereby also accepts that there are constraints on one's freedom of expression.

Although social media has resulted in further blurring of personal and professional boundaries and poses the risk of dual relationships with service users online (Reamer, 2013), this is not a new concern. The overlap between personal and professional identity and boundaries has been a focus of professional regulation and regulatory investigations even before the widespread use of social media. For example, the General Social Care Council's (GSCC) Code of Conduct stated that social workers should not:

> Behave in a way, in work or outside work, which would call into question [their] suitability to work in social care services. (Code 5.8, GSCC, 2002)

Indeed, the first case brought before the GSCC was about the application of this code and involved a social worker who had advertised herself with an escort agency. Subsequent to the GSCC investigation, the social worker received a two-year suspension from the GSCC register. This case attracted considerable attention and raised questions about social workers' privacy and the extent of overlap between personal and professional boundaries.

Social media adds a new dimension and a new layer of complexity to dual relationships and the blurring of personal and professional identities and boundaries. This raises new and complex questions in relation to practitioners' social media activities and presence, including whether social workers should use two separate social media accounts (one personal and one professional) in order to separate their personal relationships from their professional network and whether professionals *can* adequately separate their personal and professional engagements and social media posting. Although it is advisable to maintain separate personal and professional social media accounts, it is important to note that it is not possible to fully separate one's personal and professional selves; such separation is always partial and is particularly difficult if both accounts are open and public (that is, visible to everyone). Therefore, it is essential to ensure one's conduct, be it in the personal and professional sphere, does not violate the values and ethics of one's profession.

This constraint was conceded by the social worker concerned who, during the HCPC hearing, expressed regret and remorse for their actions and said they now understood that there was no separation between their persona as a professional and as a private individual.

Furthermore, freedom of speech does not justify aggressive or abusive language. Therefore, the actions and expressions of the social worker in this example were inappropriate in themselves. This was acknowledged by the Chair of HCPC panel who stated that, 'The panel accepts that there was no law against being rude or unpleasant, but there are responsibilities and standards which are voluntarily accepted and adopted by professionals'. In such cases, regulators should consider the breach of a principle and its potential effect as well as the actual actions and their actual and potential impact. Therefore, it is interesting and a point for further reflection that the HCPC panel's decision mainly focused on the impact of the social worker's actions and expressions.

Conclusion

Becoming a professional involves more than the mastery of a body of substantive knowledge and developing specific skills. It also entails developing a professional identity which, in effect, is a question of internalising appropriate professional values, ethics attitudes and behaviours. Costello (2004), in her study of law and social work students, noted that although all students were aware of the need for gaining a body of knowledge, few were aware of the need for internalising a given professional identity.

> Many students underperform at professional school precisely due to a failure to adopt and display the expected professional identity, but do not realize the nature of their problem, and seek ineffectually to improve their performance by studying harder. (Costello, 2004, p 153)

This highlights the need for separating the knowledge and skills for e-professionalism/digital professionalism from digital capabilities for social workers as digital practitioners (see Chapter 2). The Relational Boundary Scale, the identity prism and the 10 Cs risk and resilience typologies offer helpful tools and approaches for learning about relational boundaries and for assessing one's online identity as well as online risks and benefits and reflecting upon the balance between personal and professional boundaries and relationships (see Megele with Buzzi, 2017; Megele and Buzzi, 2018). However, digital and social media technologies offer unlimited possibilities and some significant and disruptive opportunities and challenges with important implication for social work practice, education and regulation. It is crucially important that social work regulation and its practice and education adequately recognise and effectively address these changes and challenges with a systemic and forward-looking perspective. Hence, this chapter concludes with a summary of some of the more salient points and recommendations for regulation and professional practice of contemporary social work:

- **Regulation should address the differences between online and offline environment, content, communication and behaviour**: As McLuhan (1964) argued, the medium is the message and, therefore, regulation should address the implications of the differences between the online and offline environment for social workers' online posts, communications, behaviours, and expressions, both in terms of guidance for professional practice and regulatory and fitness to practise investigations.
- **Blurring of boundaries and digital convergence**: The increasing overlap between personal and professional boundaries are further complicated by the digital convergence between content, context, contact/connection and communication. Although there is some overlap between the blurring of online boundaries and digital convergence and although they both add complexity to interpersonal and social relationships and interactions, they are not the same. Whereas social workers are expected to separate and maintain clear personal and professional boundaries, digital convergence is embedded in the design and nature of online posts and digital communication and cannot be fully separated. Therefore, social workers are expected to be aware and to mindfully manage its impact. Social work regulation needs to raise awareness and provide guidance relating to both of these phenomena and their implications in practice and in professional relationships.
- **Separating personal and professional social media accounts**: It is important to note that separating personal and professional social media accounts does not exonerate practitioners from professional standards. They still need to adhere to appropriate values, ethics and behaviours by both their personal and professional identities.
- **Digital literacy**: Social work regulation should promote digital literacy and require social workers as well as educators and employers to ensure that practitioners have the required knowledge and understanding of digital and

social media technologies as well as new and emerging risks (HM Government, 2018) so that social workers can use technology safely, assess online and offline risks, and provide holistic safeguarding both online and offline.

- **Combine principle-based policies with systematic and behavioural guidance**: Guidance and regulation in social work has been mostly principle-based and abstract. Although principle-based approaches lay the foundation for professionalism, it is important that this approach is complemented by systemic and behavioural guidance for practitioners. Such a combined approach will make social work regulation and professionalism visible and tangible for practitioners and will promote good practice and facilitate the achievement of professionalism in everyday practice.
- **Addressing new practice challenges and new risks**: As discussed throughout this book, social workers are faced with a host of new and emerging risks and challenges. Recognising one example of such challenges in his speech, Justice McFarlane stated that '… the erosion in the hitherto impermeable seal around the adoptive placement created by social media' requires a new approach and mind-set (McFarlane, 2017, p 17) and remains one of the most important challenges for adoption and fostering in the 21st century. Social work regulation should set the bar for professional practice when dealing with such challenges.
- **New expectations and lack of clarity in regulation**: Justice Holman's judgement ([2017] EWFC 19), cited earlier in this chapter, and the earlier cited survey and service users' feedback reflect the changing and increasing expectation among service users for social workers' use of social media for communication and in assessment of risks. Notwithstanding the RIPA (2000) and the Office of Surveillance Commissioners' Guidance (OSC, 2016), evidence suggests that there is need for greater awareness and clarity and more explicit regulation relating to digital practice in social work (Buzzi, 2019).
- **Online/digital safeguarding and holistic safeguarding**: The changing context of childhood, adulthood, communication and relationships poses significant challenges

for practice. Regulators and employers should ensure that social workers have the training, knowledge, skills and capabilities to identify and assess online and offline risks and resilience and to plan for and ensure the holistic safeguarding of people who access services. Evidence indicates that lack of due consideration and effective online/digital safeguarding by various professionals has resulted in significant harm and has had significant repercussions (see Megele with Buzzi, 2017). In a digital society, holistic safeguarding, including both offline and online/digital safeguarding, is an increasingly important challenge and an essential requirement for good practice.

- **Restorative approach to regulation and fitness to practise judgements**: Clear professional standards and strict regulation of the profession are essential for the protection of people who access services. However, professional regulation should go beyond punitive and exclusionary approaches and, when appropriate, should adopt a restorative approach to ensure that regulation and its enforcement are accompanied by appropriate and adequate guidance, training and supervision and, depending on circumstances, allow for reintegration of the practitioner into profession.
- **Clarity of actions and judgements**: Actions, judgements and decisions of regulators are an important source of learning for the profession and its professionals and therefore, should be accompanied with clear motivation and explanation to ensure learnings from the case are made explicit.
- **Resisting the media hype and ensuring proportionality**: Regulators should be protected and be able to stand against hype and inaccuracies in media reporting that can generate self-reinforcing news (Vasterman, 2005). They should also ensure that their recommendations are proportionate, their motivations explicit and their decisions grounded in critical and balanced examination of the facts and their context.
- **Clear and effective understanding of practice and technological landscape and their implications for professional regulation**: Most importantly, professional regulation and regulators should have a clear and dynamic understanding of professionalism, ethics and regulation in the context of fast-evolving technologies, communication,

relationships, practice and psychosocial landscape. This includes the recognition of the difference between online and offline environments and the need for a dynamic and contextually relevant application of ethics and regulation. Indeed, careful and critical consideration of the new context of practice is the essence of the challenge of rule setting in an increasingly digital and social world. This also requires the understanding that in a fast-changing professional, social and cultural landscape, acceptable codes of behaviour also need to evolve, and that means at times the interaction may define the rule and that the appropriate action may be counter-intuitive.

References

BASW (2012a) 'BASW Social Media Policy', Birmingham: British Association of Social Workers. Available at: http://cdn.basw.co.uk/upload/basw_34634-1.pdf

BASW (2012b) 'Why BASW developed a Social Media Policy', Birmingham: British Association of Social Workers. Available at: https://www.basw.co.uk/news/article/?id=337 (last visited December 2017).

Breyette, S. and Hill, K. (2015) 'The impact of electronic communication and social media on child welfare practice', *Journal of Technology in Human Services*, 33(4): 283–303.

Buzzi, P. (2019) *Interim results from PSW National Research and Practice Development Project*. London: King's College.

Buzzi, P. (2020a) 'Technology is never neutral: Why we should remain wary of machine learning in children's social care'. *Community Care*. Available at: https://www.communitycare.co.uk/2020/02/12/technology-never-neutral-remain-wary-machine-learning-childrens-social-care/

Buzzi, P. (2020b) 'Reflecting on the ethics of digital practice and machine learning in social care'. Presented at: Algorithmic decision-making, predictive analytics & Children's Services: Use, Ethics and Impacts. London: Nuffield Foundation.

Buzzi, P. (2020c) *Relationship based Practice in Digital Age*. London: PSW Network.

Buzzi P. and Megele C. (2012) 'Honne and Tatemae: A world dominated by a "game of masks"', in E. Christopher (ed.) *Communication Across Cultures*. London: Palgrave Macmillan.

Buzzi, P. and Megele, C. (2020) *Digital Practice and Working with Children and Young People Online*. London: PSW Network.

Clark, A. (2017) 'Digital by Default news: Salford launches ambitious 8,000 online drive'. Available at: https://www.govtechleaders.com/2017/10/23/salford-launches-ambitious-8000-online-drive/

Clark, S. (1995) *State and Status: The rise of the state and aristocratic power in Western Europe*. Montreal: McGill-Queen's University Press.

Community Care (2015) 'Social worker who sent "offensive" tweets to David Cameron found fit to practise', 11 August. Available at: https://www.communitycare.co.uk/2015/08/11/social-worker-sent-offensive-tweets-david-cameron-found-fit-practise/

Costello, C. Y. (2004). 'Changing clothes: gender inequality and professional socialization', *NWSA Journal*, 16(2): 138–55.

GSCC (2002) *Codes of Practice*. London: Department of Health.

HM Government (2018) *Working Together to Safeguard Children*. Available at: https://assets.publishing.service.gov.uk/government/uploads/system/uploads/attachment_data/file/779401/Working_Together_to_Safeguard-Children.pdf

LaMendola, W. (2010) 'Social work and social presence in an online world', *Journal of Technology in Human Services*, 28(1–2).

McFarlane, A. (2017) 'Holding the risk: The balance between child protection and the right to family life'. Bridget Lindley OBE Memorial Lecture 2017. Available at: https://www.judiciary.uk/wp-content/uploads/2017/03/lecture-by-lj-mcfarlane-20160309.pdf

McLuhan, M. (1964) *Understanding Media*. London and New York: McGraw-Hill Education.

Megele, C. (2012) 'Social care in the e-professionalism era', *The Guardian*. Available at: https://www.theguardian.com/social-care-network/2012/apr/25/eprofessionalism-social-care

Megele, C. (2014) 'Theorizing Twitter chat', *Journal of Perspective in Applied Academic Practice*, 2(2). Available at: https://jpaap.napier.ac.uk/index.php/JPAAP/article/view/106

Megele, C. (2015) *Psychosocial and Relationship-based Practice*, London: Critical Publishing.

Megele, C. (2018) *Social Media, Digital Professionalism and CPD: Strategic Briefing*. Research in Practice. Available at: https://www.researchinpractice.org.uk/children/publications/2018/december/social-media-digital-professionalism-and-cpd-strategic-briefing-2018/

Megele, C. with Buzzi, P. (2017) *Safeguarding Children and Young People Online*. Bristol: Policy Press.

Megele, C. and Buzzi, P. (2018) *Digital Professionalism and Continuous Professional Development in Social Work*. Birmingham: BASW.

OSC (2016) *Office of Surveillance Commissioners Procedures and Guidance* (July). Available at: https://www.gov.uk/government/organisations/office-of-surveillance-commissioners

Polignano, M., de Gemma, M., Narducci, F. and Semeraro, G. (2017) 'Do you feel blue? Detection of negative feeling from social media', Conference of Italian Association of Artificial Intelligence, available at: https://www.researchgate.net/publication/320875235_Do_You_Feel_Blue_Detection_of_Negative_Feeling_from_Social_Media.

Reamer, F. (2013) 'The digital and electronic revolution in social work: Rethinking the meaning of ethical practice', *Ethics and Social Welfare*, 7(1): 2–19.

Sage, T. and Sage, M. (2016) 'Social media use in child welfare practice', *Advances in Social Work*, 17(1): 93–112. Available at: https://www.researchgate.net/publication/301640235_Social_Media_Use_in_Child_Welfare_Practice

Suler, J. R. (2004) 'The online disinhibition effect', *Cyberpsychology & Behavior*, 7(3): pp 321–6.

Turner, A. (2019) 'Facebook surveillance becoming 'normalised' in some social work teams, research concludes', *Community Care*. Available at: https://www.communitycare.co.uk/2019/10/24/facebook-surveillance-normalised-among-social-workers-study-concludes/

Vasterman, P. (2005) 'Media-hype self-reinforcing news waves, journalistic standards and the construction of social problems', *European Journal of Communication*, 20(4): 508–30.

Weber, M. (1978) 'Classes, status groups and parties' in *Weber: Selections in Translation*, W.G. Runciman (ed) and E. Matthews (trans), pp 43–61. Cambridge: Cambridge University Press.

9

Future technology and social work and social care practice and education

Claudia Megele and Peter Buzzi

Introduction

As changes in technology create new ways of communicating, relating, living and being, they offer new opportunities and also generate new risks and ethical challenges. Indeed, technology impacts and transforms every aspect of people's lives, including the meaning of childhood, parenting, friendships, relationships, education, work, play, leisure, privacy, identity, equality and the very notion of humanness. Previous chapters have examined the different ways technology impacts social work and social care practice and education. This concluding chapter briefly examines some of the ways the developments in digital and social media technologies may impact and change social work and social care practice and education in coming years.

Evolution of the web

Although most conversations about the web are focused on web 2.0, part of the technology for web 3.0 and web 4.0 are already in use today. The evolution of the web has a significant impact on every aspect of life, including health, social work and social care. Let us briefly consider what we mean by the successive versions of the web.

Web 1.0 was the web of content and documents. It was mostly used as an information focused, one-way communication tool. It was built around the 'home page' and accumulation and ownership of content. At its best, it functioned like a telephone directory or the *Encyclopaedia Britannica.*

Web 2.0 is the 'social web' of communication and people. It is a two-way medium that is interactive and community-focused, and is built around sharing of content and information. Social media, wikis, mashups, and different SNS are examples of web 2.0.

Web 3.0 or the 'internet of things' is the web of context and data, focused on individuals and personalisation. Web 3.0 is built around Life Streams and user behaviour and offers contextual content. Google search is an example of web 3.0. With web 3.0 everything from the cooker, coffee maker and toaster to light bulbs and car keys, not just phones and computers, will have microchips, sensors and IP addresses and be connected in a web. This means they can be managed remotely and stream data to services that can improve and be optimised over time using that data. These capabilities will transform health and social care, allowing better and more person-centred e-services, e-intervention, and e-care.

Web 4.0 is the web of thoughts, artificial intelligence (AI) and direct brain link. It is still in the making but should be with us in the next decade or so. It is the 'intelligent web' that offers read-write-execution concurrency. This means systems will be able to recognise stimuli, gather the relevant data to make an informed decision, decide appropriate response and course of action, and then execute that decision and action. Web 4.0 will interface with its users in multiple ways and through normal speaking/conversation ('natural language'). Applications of web 4.0 vary from personal assistants to robots and cybernetics. Alexa, Cortana, Google Now and Siri are current examples of web 4.0. Web 4.0 will transform every phase of life and, as it further blurs the boundaries of 'living' and of human and machine, it presents the most empowering and yet the greatest challenge so far for social policy and social care.

Table 9.1 summarises the evolution of the web so far and its impact on several areas of interest.

Web 5.0 is the 'web of emotions'. It is expected to be the open-link intelligent and emotional web that uses neurotechnology to perceive and interact with human emotions. An example is www.wefeelfine.org which maps users' emotions (through headsets, users will interact with content that responds to their emotions or changes in facial expression). Specially designed avatars and apps are already helping people who experience emotional or mental health difficulties better manage their feelings and difficult experiences. In the future, these may be used to provide a personalised, contextual and emotionally appropriate interface. For example, your phone, television or wearable device will recognise your mood and will be able to react in supportive and soothing ways, alleviating everyday stress or mental health distress.

Artificial intelligence (AI) and robotics in social care

AI and robotics are perhaps the most significant technological development, with potential for greater impact than that of the industrial revolution. The applications of AI and their effects are truly far-reaching and span from early-years help and education to child protection and adoption, from health care to police investigations, from Google search to driverless cars, from companionship to specialist diagnosis and patient care, and from risk management and safeguarding to matching children and foster carers. These technologies present unprecedented opportunities and challenges for every profession and every aspect of human experience and wellbeing.

For example, machine learning and predictive analysis are being used for more comprehensive and accurate medical diagnosis and patient information management, while robots are already providing support in health and social care for people and their family and carers (such as Paro or Robear, described later). One report found that AI could identify evidence-based therapies for 30% of cancer patients that were not identified by their oncologists; in this sense the AI system outperformed the specialist doctors (BBC, 2020).

Table 9.1: The impact of the web and digital and social media technologies

Web evolution	**Web 1.0**	**Web 2.0**	**Web 3.0**	**Web 4.0**
Use of data	Mainly read-only	Widely read-write	Portable and personal	AI and personal assistants
The main focus of postings	Information focus	Community focus	Person and data focus	Read-write-execute concurrency
Known as	Web of content	Web of communication	Web of context	Web of thoughts and direct brain link
Organisational perspective	Home page	Blogs, wikis, SNS, mashups	Life Stream/Waves	AI automation
Change in web content	Owning content	Sharing content	Contextualising content	Merging of content and application
Software focus	One-way communication	Interactive web of sharing	Smart apps	Intelligent and cognitive capabilities
Interface with users	Web forms	Web apps	Smart apps	AI and humanoid interface
Organisation of data	Directories	Tagging and hashtags	User behaviour	Behavioural profiles and thought maps
Measure of activity	Page views	Cost per click	User engagement	Thought sharing and connecting with others
Example of software	Britannica Online	Wikipedia	The Semantic Web	Alexa, Cortana, Google Now, Siri

(continued)

Table 9.1: The impact of the web and digital & social media technologies (continued)

Web evolution	Web 1.0	Web 2.0	Web 3.0	Web 4.0
Impact on privacy	Limited non-interactive data mostly private until shared	Posts are 'social' and interactive but can be made private	Surveillance culture and virtual absence of privacy, technology registers every action, consumption, location and behaviour	Profiling users' behaviour, personality, digital body language including actions and lack of action, mood, and so on
Impact on identity	Identity understood as mostly offline	Liminal (online and offline) narratives and identity	Multiple data points online and offline that create detailed user profiles	Predictive capability to assess and interact based on person's needs, thoughts, emotions and behaviour
Impact on behaviour and thinking	Increasing reliance on digital in everyday life	Web is an integral part of people's lives and identities	Smart devices and wearables extend individual control and capabilities	Use of androids and robotics; cybernetics enable use and absorption of technology as extension of human body
Impact on children	Relatively limited impact on childhood and children	Increasing and widespread use of tech and emergence of 'cyborg childhood'	Children are born digital and raised social increasing use of tech in childcare	Technology and AI guide parenting, use of robotics for surrogate parenting
Impact on young people	Relatively limited impact	Changing communication and transformation of identity, relationships and social capital	Indispensable for young people's learning, development, identity and digital citizenship	Virtual and global are refocused on physical and local in productive ways

(continued)

Table 9.1: The impact of the web and digital & social media technologies (continued)

Web evolution	Web 1.0	Web 2.0	Web 3.0	Web 4.0
Impact on parenting	Little use of web in parenting	Increasingly challenged by technology and its impact on children and childhood	Use of apps to assist parenting including ability for surveillance to monitor and block children's activity	Use of intelligent and predictive technology to support and facilitate parenting and surrogate parenting
Impact on local government	New channel for non-interactive information sharing	Interactive information sharing, crowd sourcing and collective decision making	Co-production of practice and e-governance and public behavioural modification	Collective governance, advanced behavioural management
Impact on health and social care	Increased use of email and other private channels for interprofessional working and information sharing	Use of online communities, support groups, online therapy and interactive communication	Use of wearables and assistive technology for e-support, e-meetings, e-interventions and co-production of services	Predictive and intelligent, person-centred and person-led support and intervention
Impact on support and safeguarding practice	Increased use of email and other private channels for interprofessional working and information sharing	New safeguarding risks and opportunities, digital safeguarding and need for holistic safeguarding	Integrated safeguarding and innovative use of data points and apps, e-support and e-interventions	Predictive support and safeguarding including: use of machine learning to identify and remove abusive content; use of AI in matching children and foster carers; care analytics and risk management and decision support systems

Source: Megele with Buzzi, 2017

AI can also support social work and social care practice and decision making. For example, AI can help and support practitioners and organisations in matching children and young people with foster carers in order to ensure a better fit. AI can support youth justice practice and help work with adolescents who are experiencing a range of difficulties. Furthermore, AI-driven care analytics can support practitioners and managers in managing risks, making better informed decisions and more holistic safeguarding, while ensuring a clear line of sight from strategic leadership to frontline practice. For example, Essex County Council uses machine learning to produce anonymised aggregate data, at community level, of children who may not be ready for school by their fifth birthday. This data is then shared with parents and services who are part of the project to inform their funding decisions or changes to practice as need be. This is a good example of positive use of machine learning and predictive analysis to support children and families that is preventive and yet empowering for both parents and professionals.

Another example of AI is the use of Paro in the NHS to support people living with dementia. Paro is a robot made by Takanori Shibata at Japan's National Institute of Advanced Industrial Science and Technology (AIST). Paro was first exhibited in 2001 and a handmade version of Paro as a stuffed animal in form of a harp seal has been sold by Shibata's company in Japan since 2004. Paro serves as a 'transitional object' and its use has been experimented on in a number of countries; for example, in 2004 Paro was used in Japan and Sweden for supporting autistic children and children with disabilities. Since 2014, it has been used by the NHS to research better support for people living with dementia. A 'transitional object' is a surrogate that symbolises the bond between people (for example, between infant and the primary caregiver):

> … at times when such bond is missing or lacking. Transitional objects may take a variety of forms (e.g. rags, dolls, or other toys/objects or even a word, or the Linus blanket). Through the creation of the transitional object the infant creates its first not-me object that functions at the will and control

> of the child. The transitional object offers a symbolic medium that serves as the locus for projections of the person's affections, insecurities and anxieties, and offers an illusion of the attachment bonds that can contain and attenuate the individual's anxiety. (Megele, 2015, p 26)

Robots and apps can also help children with their development, serve as their personal assistant, and offer intelligent and contextual support and companionship. They can also support and assist parents and other adults, including those who experience mental health difficulties, trauma, pain or other challenges.

Robear is another Japanese robot that combines strengths with accuracy and gentleness and can perform support tasks such as lifting patients from their bed into a wheelchair or can assist patients who are able to stand up but required help to do so.

Use of technology to better support people who access services

Such transformations and the increasing merging of human and machine occur on multiple levels and go beyond the physical (bionics) to involve the extending of human thought, feelings and capabilities. Indeed, our thinking about and understanding of care and safeguarding are extended and transformed by these technologies. For example, instead of static parental control software that allows parents to block access to harmful or age-inappropriate websites for children, use of AI will enable parents to provide dynamic and contextual protection for children and young people based on sophisticated supervision and protection software that apply parental preferences to patterns of behaviour and interactions in an interactive manner.

Many adult social care services offer or encourage use of Amazon's Alexa and the Amazon Echo system to complement support from human carers. This is particularly helpful since people do not need to have any technical knowledge or IT preparation and can verbally interact with Alexa in natural language. Alexa can engage in conversation or can be used to offer reminders or other relevant information (e.g. when the supporter will arrive or when to take the next medication), answer various questions, contact friends or family, keep in touch with community, control the person's living environment (e.g. turning lights on or off or controlling the front door etc.), encourage walking or other exercise to keep fit, and so on. Alexa can also be used to simplify check-in and administration for carers. The feedback from service users experience of Alexa has been very positive including people finding Alexa 'thoroughly enjoyable' and 'good company'.

Digital and biotechnological convergence

One of the most important impacts and continuing trends in social technologies is the increasing digital and technological convergence between content, context, contact, connection and behaviour (Megele with Buzzi, 2017; Buzzi and Megele, 2020). These changes will result in continued shifts in boundaries, with their ethical and practical implications for the definition of professional roles, personal and professional boundaries and the safeguarding of data and privacy. The increase in data sharing, behavioural analysis, user profiling and other ways of learning and understanding individuals will dominate access to services and will result in continued and further transformation of privacy; with digital devices becoming our virtual and individual assistants, there will be little if anything about anyone that will not be available and known to Apple, Amazon, Google, Facebook, Microsoft or other major SNS or providers of online services. This is a significant change, as access to most services, including basic services, will require sharing of personal and behavioural data that result in continued dilution of individual privacy and its increasing displacement and replacement by new forms and notions of privacy and new notions of trust. Hence, there is an urgent need for a more critical, proactive and creative notion of privacy, confidentiality, trust and professionalism and their ramifications.

As described in Chapter 2, digital convergence is an example of such shifting and transformation of boundaries that poses new and immediate challenges for safeguarding practice. For example, technology enables birth parents of adopted or looked after children to retrace and contact their children online and often in an unsupervised manner. Indeed, as acknowledged by Justice McFarlane (2017, p. 17) '… the erosion of the hitherto impermeable seal around the adoptive placement created by social media' requires a new approach and mind-set and remains one of the most urgent and important challenges for adoption and fostering services.

Dominance of apps and the need for further transparency

Continued changes in SNS and social technologies will lead to different and new forms of engagement, sociality, friendship and coproduction which will be facilitated through apps. Even access to basic information, activities, communication and relationships will increasingly require the use of apps and digital technologies. Apps cover a vast range of services, from finding a public toilet to health care and medical consultation and diagnosis, and from education to employment, and from games and leisure to team working and relationships, and so on. However, at the moment there is a lack of transparency; combined with the absence of relevant legislation this can lead to situation similar to what happened with Uber app. Security researchers revealed that, in order to improve functionality between Uber's app and the Apple Watch for an Apple presentation in March 2015, Apple allowed Uber to use a powerful tool that could record a user's iPhone screen, even if Uber's app was only running in the background. This means that Uber could access, observe and record everything a user did and everything the user saw on their Apple watch screen. Just imagine having someone looking over your shoulder and recording everything you do on your computer; that was the permission granted to Uber for the presentation by Apple and was not revoked after the presentation. Only after the researchers discovered the tool, Uber said it is no longer in use and will be removed from the app (*The Telegraph*, 2017). In February 2020, the UK Government announced that they will appoint Ofcom as an internet watchdog, giving it the ability to fine social media companies that do not protect users from harmful content (*The Guardian*, 2020).

This is an example of a hasty solution between two companies using a long-shot approach to meet their own objectives without regard for individual data and privacy. Appropriate and more explicit and proactive legislation is required to ensure that companies are held accountable when they infringe on individual privacy and digital citizenship.

Truth and authenticity

Notwithstanding their great positive potential, SNS can also be used in damaging ways. For example, the emergence and spread of false news, 'fake news' websites and the manipulative use of SNSs combined with behavioural data analytics allow micro-targeting, which has been used to influence public audiences opinions and behaviours. The US presidential election in 2016 is a prime example. This threatens the foundation of democracies based on free and informed choice. The Oxford Dictionary's Word of the Year for 2016, 'post-truth', encapsulates the challenge associated with these developments; Oxford Dictionary defines this as 'relating to or denoting circumstances in which objective facts are less influential in shaping public opinion than appeals to emotion and personal belief'. These developments highlight the need for a proactive approach to digital citizenship.

Wearable technology

Wearable technology will offer seamless support and services, lead to further merging of human and technology, and reshape every aspect of caring, support and safeguarding. This will transform social care and social work practice, education and services. However, this also raises the question of whether access to such technologies would be supported by public funding, especially for technologies that can help meet individuals' basic needs or transform individuals' health, longevity, quality of life and wellbeing. The absence of such funding will only exacerbate already significant social inequalities.

For example, by monitoring specific health, medical, bio-physical, or emotional indicators/factors, people can monitor and manage their own wellbeing and receive tailor-made medical, health and wellbeing reports, information and advice on their phone or other digital devices. This also enables practitioners to provide better and more targeted early intervention as well as e-intervention (ranging from reminders for taking one's medication to e-intervention and remotely administering specific medicines, to emotional support) to minimise and mitigate crisis situations and enhance people's quality of life. These approaches can be empowering for people as they allow greater control and self-management with respect to their health and social care needs.

Some of the trends that are in the making and that seem to be a clear direction of travel for health and social care sector include:

- Individual health records will increasingly contain and be linked to data from the individual and their various wearable devices as well as other sources.
- There will be increasingly integrated health and social care solutions that are built around the needs and preferences of the people who access services.
- Data, solutions and services will go beyond 'wearables' and will be comprised of a host of other e-interventions, approaches and techniques. These include skin patches, pills and contact lenses with chips, and other e-monitoring, e-support, and e-intervention devices, techniques and approaches either wearable or embedded in the individual's body.
- Most importantly, wearable and other digital and social technologies will give individuals greater and better health and social care solutions, expert advice and more information for decisions, more and better choices, and greater control over their health and social care while enhancing their quality of life and wellbeing.

Conclusion

As highlighted in Table 9.1, the evolutions of the web and digital and social technologies will continue to have a significant impact on every aspect of life, health and social care. However, this technological change and its impact in society are also accompanied by new ways of caring, sharing and being. This entails both opportunities as well as ethical, practical and humane challenges. Therefore, it is essential that social work and social care practitioners are able to enhance their digital professionalism and ability to support, guide and safeguard children, adults and families in an increasingly mediated digital world. This is what motivated the authors to draw on the wisdom of various practitioners, experts and leaders in social work and social care in this book to offer a digital journey that provides an overview of social media and its impact and implications for social work practice and education.

References

BBC (2020) 'AI "outperforms" doctors diagnosing breast cancer', 2 January. Available at: https://www.bbc.co.uk/news/health-50857759

Buzzi, P. and Megele, C. (2020) *Digital Practice and Working with Children and Young People Online*. London: PSW Network.

McFarlane, A. (2017) 'Holding the risk: The balance between child protection and the right to family life'. Available at: https://www.judiciary.gov.uk/wp-content/uploads/2017/03/lecture-by-lj-mcfarlane-20160309.pdf

Megele, C. (2015) *Psychosocial and Relationship based Practice*. London: Critical Publishing.

Megele, C. with Buzzi, P. (2017) *Safeguarding Children and Young People Online*. Bristol: Policy Press.

The Guardian (2020) 'What powers will Ofcom have to regulate the internet?', 12 February. Available at: https://www.theguardian.com/media/2020/feb/12/what-powers-ofcom-have-regulate-internet-uk

The Telegraph (2017) 'Apple gave Uber 'disturbing' access to users' iPhone data', 6 October. Available at: https://www.telegraph.co.uk/technology/2017/10/06/uber-app-could-secretly-record-iphone-users-screens/

Index

Note: Page numbers in *italics* refer to figures or tables.

10 Cs risk and resilience toolkit 34, 51–4, 66, 75–6, 77, 187–8
#BabyRP 71–2
@MHChat 117, 126, 160, 168
#notinmyname 146
#OneBigDebate 143–6, 147
#SocialWork 159
#SWSCmedia 162
@SWSCmedia 126, 157–64
  between community and network 165–7
  lessons learnt 170–2
  multilogue conversations 164–5
  professional identity 168

A

adopted children 79–82, 192, 216
adoption 193
adult social work and social care
  adult social care
    apps 107–8
    dementia case study 104–7
    health and wellbeing 99–100
    social media use 97–8
  adult social work 93, 108–9
    digital storytelling 101–3
adult supervision 67
adults
  relationships and social capital 100–1
  social media use 94–7, 115–16
alcohol 73
Alzheimer's 102
Amazon Alexa and Echo 97, 180, 214–15
anonymity 42–3, 44, 65, 71, 83, 196
antipsychotic medication 120
Apple 216
apps 107–8, 119–21, 214, 216–17
artificial intelligence (AI) 7, 8, 45, 97, 209, 213–15
assessment diamond 62–3
asynchronocity 43
asynchronous communication 70–1
audience 52
authenticity 52, 189, 217
authority 44–5
autism 103–4
avatar therapy 120–2

B

#BabyRP 71–2
Barnardos 64, 75
benign disinhibition 41
biotechnological convergence 215–16
birth parents 79–82, 192, 193, 216
boundaries
  children's online engagement 67
  personal and professional 2, 26–7, 30, 128, 197–8, 200, 215
  between self and others 28
Bourdieu, Pierre 100
Breyette, S. 190
British Association of Social Workers (BASW) 46, 177–8, 181
Brown, J.S. 165
bullying 48, 170
  see also cyberbullying
Buzzi, P. 179, 180, 187, 190–1
bystanders 48

C

Case, S. 138
Channel 4 News 79–80

Cheal, S. 137
Child Exploitation and Online Protection Command (CEOP) 84
child sex offences 64
child sexual abuse 82–4
child sexual offenders 42, 82
child welfare workers 189–90
ChildLine 78
Children Act 1989 85
children and young people
  10 Cs risk and resilience toolkit 34, 51-54, 66, 75–6, 77, 187–8
  communication with birth parents 79–82, 192, 216
  cyberbullying 77–9, 135
  dark play 71–2
  development, relationships and identity 69–71
  digital citizenship 62, 66, 68, 85
  digital immigrants 32, 94, 96
  digital natives 32, 94, 96
  expectations of social workers 179–81
  geographical v. online space 139–43
  holistic safeguarding *63*, 84–5, 193, 201–3
  mental health problems 65, 123–4
  online anonymity 42, 71
  online grooming 82–4, 134
  online identity 68–9
  play 66–7
  as resource for decision making 182
  risk 65, 67–9, 191–3
  robotics 214
  sexting 72–7, 134, 135
  social media use 64–6, 190–1
  technology 61–2
Children's Commissioner 86
civic engagement 118–19
Clark, A. 181
cocoon effect 45–6, 196
collaboration and coproduction 125–8
commercial exploitation 54
communication
  asynchronous 70–1
  with birth parents 79–82, 192, 216
  digital 138
  multilogue 164–5
  non-verbal 29
  offline 24–30, 164
  online 24–30, 41–6
  textual 43–4, 103
communities of practice 155–7, 169–73
  @SWSCmedia 126, 157–64
    between community and network 165–7
    identity processes 168
    lessons learnt 170–2
    multilogue conversations 164–5
  and professional identity 167–9
'Communities versus networks' (Fiore) 166
community 156, 166
community action 143–6
Community Care 197
compatibility 52
conduct 53–4
confidentiality 53
connected co-presence 38
connection 52–3
Connelly, Peter 184–5
Conradie, L. 137, 138–9
consent 137, 149, 188–9
consumption 54
contact 53
content 53
context 52
continuous professional development (CPD) 127
co-presence 38
coproduction 49–51, 171
Counter Extremism Strategy 134
Covert Human Intelligence Sources (CHIS) 187
curating 51
cyberbullying 73, 77–9, 135
cyborg identity 9

D

dark play 71–2
Darke, S. 137
dementia 102, 104–7

digilanguage 28–30, 43
'Digital by default' agenda (UK Government, 2016) 6
digital citizenship 11
practitioners 47–9, 51, 86
Salford City Council 180
young people 62, 66, 68, 85
digital communication 138
digital convergence 215–16
digital enablement 11
digital exclusion 66, 180
digital footprint 25–6
digital immigrants 32, 96
digital inequality 11–12, 66, 95, 122
digital life storybooks 102
digital literacy 200–1
digital lives 5–8
digital natives 32, 96
digital ombudsman 86
digital presence and engagement 51–4
digital professionalism *see* e-professionalism (digital professionalism)
digital residents 32–3
digital rights 62, 66, 68
digital safeguarding 85, 191–3, 201–2
see also online safeguarding
digital storytelling 101–3
digital visitors 32–3
disability 103–7
displacement hypothesis 101
dissociative anonymity 42–3, 44, 65
Ditch the Label 135
diversity 45
domains of information sharing 30–3, 35–6
drugs 73
Duguid, P. 165
dynamic risk factors 78–9

E

echo chambers 45, 46
e-interventions 119–20, 218
e-learning 127
enhanced capabilities 51
e-professionalism (digital professionalism)
definitions 23–4, 178
domains of information sharing 30–3
and ethics 20–3, 193–5
freedom of speech 195–8
knowledge, skills and capabilities 46–51
learning points 55–6
online communication
differences between offline and 24–30
distinctive characteristics 41–6
e-professionalism (continued)
online presence and engagement 51–4
Social Media Activity and Reflection Tool (SMART) 33–7
social presence 37–41
training and support 192–3
Erikson, E.H. 70
e-safety 85
Essex County Council 213
Eternime 8
ethical recognition 51
ethics
communities of practice 171
dementia 106–7
and e-professionalism 20–3, 56
surveillance 187
young people 137, 148–9, 150–1

F

Facebook
dementia case study 104–7
e-professionalism 20–3
London riots 2011 135
recruitment 97
Social Media Activity and Reflection Tool (SMART) 35–6
US elections 2010 136
fake news 217
Fiore, Dal 166
foster children 79–82
freedom of speech 195–8
friending 65

G

gangs 144, 145
gender 78
gender roles 76
General Social Care Council (GSCC) 197–8
geographical v. online space 139–43
Google search 9, 64, 181, 185
grooming *see* online grooming
Gunawardena, C. 37

H

Haines, K. 138
Hampshire County Council 180
Haraway, Donna 9
harm, triangle of 67
hashes 84
HCPC fitness to practice hearings 2, 20–3, 26–7, 184, 193–9
health and social care 99–100
  see also adult social care
health intervention technologies 119–20
  artificial intelligence (AI) 209, 213–14
  avatar therapy 120–2
hierarchy 44, 126, 166
Hill, K. 190
Hodgkin, P. 117–18
holistic safeguarding *63*, 84–5, 193, 201–2
Holman, James 10, 193, 201
home visits 180
Hughes, N. 138
Human Rights Act 1998 186

I

identity
  cyborg 9
  online 51–5, 65, 68–9, 83
  professional 167–9
  social media 7
  young people 69–71
identity construction 167–9
information sharing 31–2
information technology (IT) 2–3, 3–4
internet access 11, 67
  see also digital inequality
internet use 95–6
Internet Watch Foundation 84
intersectional analysis 95
intersectionality 94
invisibility 43–4

K

knowledge generation *161*, 162
knowledge pooling 51

L

Lam, A. 166
language *see* digilanguage; motivational language
Le Cornu, Alison 32–3
levelling effect 44
life story books 80, 102
Liveson.org 8
London riots 2011 135–6, 146
looked-after children 79–82, 216
LSE 135–6

M

machine learning 45
marijuana 73
McFarlane, A. 10, 82, 201, 216
media 157, 202
Megele, C. 179, 180, 187, 190–1
mental health 113–14, 119–22, 124–5
  avatar therapy 120–2
  civic engagement 118–19
  digital inequality 122
  social media as reflective space 116–18
  young people 65, 123–4
Mental Health Chat 126
mental health social work 114
  collaboration and coproduction 125–8
  health intervention technologies 119–20
  practice recommendations 128–30
  risks and opportunities 123–4
  safeguarding 124–5
  social networks 114–16
mindline 52
mobile technologies 2–3
mobility 156
moral disengagement 79

motivational language 34, 187
multilogue conversations 164–5
multitasking 49
Myhomehelper 107

N

negotiation 51
Net Aware 84
networking 51
networks of practice 165, 166, 167
NHS Open Dialogue 116
non-individuated co-presence 38
#notinmyname 146
Nourish 107–8
NSPCC 75, 82, 84

O

Ofcom 64, 86, 95, 216
Office of National Statistics (ONS) 11
Office of Surveillance Commissioners (OSC) 185–7
offline behaviour 136
offline communication 24–30, 164
older people
  apps 107–8
  dementia case study 104–7
  digital immigrants 32, 96
  social media use 94
#OneBigDebate 143–6, 147
online communication 24–30, 41–6
  see also textual communication; virtual communication
online communities 117, 126, 142–3, 167, 170–3
  see also communities of practice
online disinhibition effect 41–2, 65, 196
online footprint 8
online forums 127–8
online grooming 82–4, 134
online identity 51–4, 65, 68–9, 83
online information 184–91
online learning 127
online presence and engagement 51–4
online safeguarding 84, 85, 124–5, 201–2
  see also digital safeguarding
online v. geographical space 139–43
others
  boundaries between self and 28
  sense of 38

P

parallel co-presence 38
parental control 214
Paro 213
peer groups 77
peer interactions 70
peer socialisation 65
peer support 117
personal and professional boundaries 2, 26–7, 30, 128, 197–8, 200, 215
personal disclosure 53
personal domain 31, 32, 35
Personal Learning Network (PLN) 169
personality 79
Pew Research Center 94
phobias 121
play 66–7
  dark 71–2
post-truth 217
power 44–5, 126, 137
power imbalance 181–2
Prensky, M. 32, 96
Principal Children and Families Social Workers (PCFSW) network 46–7
privacy 137, 149, 186, 190, 216–17
privacy settings 22, 27–8, 35–6, 53, 186
private domain 31, 32, 35–6
private information 186, 188–9
professional and personal boundaries 2, 26–7, 30, 128, 197–8, 200, 215
Professional Capabilities Framework (PCF) 181
professional domain 31, 32, 35
professional identity 167–9
professional practice 200–2
professional responsibility 195–8
professionalism 182, 183–4, 191, 199

see also e-professionalism (digital professionalism)
professions 181–2
projected presence 38
psychosis 120, 121
public domain 31, 32, 35–6, 137
Puras, Dainius 118

R

RallyRound 107
rape 82
reflective cycle of knowledge generation *161*, 162
regulation 86, 183–4, 200–3
see also social media policy
Regulation of Investigatory Powers Act 2000 (RIPA) 185, 186, 187
residents 32–3
riots 2011 135–6, 146
risk
10 Cs risk and resilience toolkit 34, 51–4, 66, 75–6, 77, 187–8
mental health social work 123–5
ROAG colour coding 37
young people 65, 67–9, 191–3
risk factors 78–9
risk-taking behaviours 73, 78–9
ROAG colour coding 37
Robear 214
robotics 209, 213–14
role-play 71–2

S

safe zones 67
safeguarding *63*, 67, 84–5, 124–5, 191–3, 201–2
Sage, T. and M. 189–90
Salford City Council 180
schizophrenia 120, 121
self-boundaries 28
self-disclosure 70–1
Serious and Organised Crime Strategy 134
service users
expectations of social workers 179–81
online information 184–91
power imbalance between social workers and 181–2
see also specific client groups
sexting 72–7, 134, 135
sexual offenders 82–3
Share Aware 75
Short, J. 37
simulation 49
Skills for Care 97
Skype 36
smoking 73
social analytics 7
social augmentation hypothesis 100, 101
'social by default' 9, 27, 30
social capital 52–3, 100, 115, 118
social care *see* adult social care; health and social care
'Social Care Curry' 126
social isolation 101
social media
importance for young people's development 69–71
as mediated reflective space 116–18
Social Media Activity and Reflection Tool (SMART) 33–7, 187–8
social presence 37–41
social media companies 86
social media identities 7
see also online identity
social media information 184–91
social media mapping 33–41
social media policy 46, 147, 177–8
social media presence 51–4
social media searches 185
social media technologies 2–3, *210–12*
benefits 3–4
embedded nature of 8–10
impact on social work practice 10–11
impact throughout lifespan 5–8
social media use
adult social care 97–8
adults 94–7, 115–16
changing expectations in social work 179–81
older people 94
young people 64–6, 190–1
social network theory 116
social networks 114–16, 165, 166, 167

social presence 7, 37–41
#SocialWork 159
social work
  expectations of social media use in 179–81
  impact of technology on 10–11
Social Work and Media (@SWSCmedia) 126, 157–64
  between community and network 165–7
  lessons learnt 170–2
  multilogue conversations 164–5
  professional identity 168
social work regulation 183–4
  see also social media policy
social work values 3–5
social workers
  digital citizenship 47–9, 51, 85–6
  online risks and digital safeguarding 191–3
  power imbalance between service users and 181–2
  service users' online information 184–91
solipsistic introjection 28
space, geographical v. online 139–43
space/place 32–3
splitting 80
static risk factors 78
status 44–5, 126
stereotypes 96, 108
stigma 118
stigmatisation 96, 108
storytelling *see* digital storytelling
Suler, J. 41
supervision 67
surveillance 185–6
#SWSCmedia 162
@SWSCmedia 126, 157–64
  between community and network 165–7
  lessons learnt 170–2
  multilogue conversations 164–5
  professional identity 168

T

technology 8–10, 61–2
  see also health intervention technologies; information technology (IT); social media technologies; wearable technology
tele-interventions 120
textual communication 43–4, 103
tools 32–3
toxic disinhibition 41
training 147–8, 192–3
transitional objects 213–14
transmedia appropriation 51
transparency 216–17
transparency problem 9–10
triangle of harm 67
trolling 170
truth 217
Twitter 97
  #OneBigDebate 144, 145, 147
  @SWSCmedia 126, 157–64
    between community and network 165–7
    lessons learnt 170–2
    multilogue conversations 164–5
    professional identity 168
  Liveson.org 8
  London riots 2011 135–6
Twitter speech 161

U

Uber 216
United Nations Convention on the Rights of the Child (UNCRC) 85, 137
United Nations (UN) 118
US elections 2010 136
US elections 2016 217

V

values 3–5, 79
virtual communication 138
virtual reality *see* avatar therapy
visitors 32–3

W

wearable technology 217–18
web evolution 207–9, *210–12*
Webber, M. 116
Weber, M. 181
White, David 32–3
Wilson, Tallulah 68–9
Working Together to Safeguard Children (HM Government, 2018) 180–1
World Health Organization (WHO) 99

Y

young people
  10 Cs risk and resilience toolkit 34, 51–4, 66, 75–6, 77, 187–8
  communication with birth parents 79–82, 192, 216
  cyberbullying 77–9, 135
  dark play 71–2
  development, relationships and identity 69–71
  digital citizenship 62, 66, 68, 85
  digital natives 32, 96
  expectations of social workers 179–80
  geographical v. online space 139–43
  holistic safeguarding *63*, 84–5, 193
  mental health problems 65, 123–4
  online anonymity 42, 71
  online grooming 82–4, 134
  online identity 68–9
  play 66–7
  as resource for decision making 182
  risk 65, 67–9, 191–3
  sexting 72–7, 134, 135
  social media use 64–6, 190–1
  technology 61–2
youth involvement 143–6
youth justice 133–7, 137–8, 150–1
youth justice practice 146–9
youth workers 137, 138–9